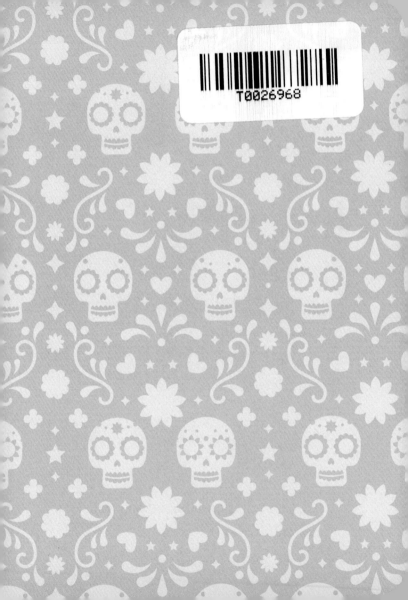

LLEWELLYN'S

Little Book of

THE DAY OF
THE DEAD

© Marcela Robledo

Jaime Gironés (Mexico City) was born in 1989. He has followed the Wiccan path since he was thirteen years old. He writes about spirituality, magic, minority religions, myths, and Witchcraft, focusing on Mexico and Latin America. He works in customer service and social media. He has collaborated as an international columnist for *The Wild Hunt*, a daily news site for Pagans, Heathens, Wiccans, Witches, and polytheists.

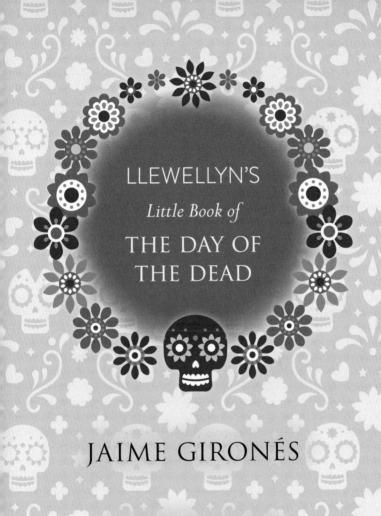

LLEWELLYN'S
Little Book of
THE DAY OF
THE DEAD

JAIME GIRONÉS

LLEWELLYN PUBLICATIONS
WOODBURY, MINNESOTA

FIRST EDITION
First Printing, 2021

Cover cartouche by Freepik
Cover design by Shira Atakpu
Interior art elements designed by the Llewellyn Art Department
Interior illustrations by Sara Koncilja

Llewellyn Publications is a registered trademark of Llewellyn Worldwide Ltd.

Library of Congress Cataloging-in-Publication Data (Pending)

Llewellyn Worldwide Ltd. does not participate in, endorse, or have any authority or responsibility concerning private business transactions between our authors and the public.

All mail addressed to the author is forwarded, but the publisher cannot, unless specifically instructed by the author, give out an address or phone number.

Any internet references contained in this work are current at publication time, but the publisher cannot guarantee that a specific location will continue to be maintained. Please refer to the publisher's website for links to authors' websites and other sources.

Llewellyn Publications
A Division of Llewellyn Worldwide Ltd.
2143 Wooddale Drive
Woodbury, MN 55125-2989
www.llewellyn.com

Printed in China

To Miss Meche, who taught me
to appreciate the Day of the Dead.

To my grandmothers, Yolanda and Raquel, who shared with me
their love when they were alive and still do so in spirit.

To all my ancestors, to the lives they lived, and to their legacy.
May we meet again.

Acknowledgments

I would like to first thank Heather Greene, for thinking of me for this project and her constant patience and guidance. I deeply appreciate that you believe in me, Heather; you have believed in me even during times when I am not able to believe in myself. You are a candle of light that illuminates my path. Thank you as well to Lauryn Heineman and all of Llewellyn's team involved in this project; my eternal appreciation for helping me take this project from an idea to the reader's hands. I would also like to thank Andrés, my life partner, for his love and support, and my sisters, my brother, and my parents, for sharing with me our love for the Day of the Dead.

Contents

Actividades (Activities and Exercises)

ix

AUTHOR'S NOTE

As this is a book about a traditional Mexican holiday, *Día de los Muertos*, I find it necessary to mention the topic of cultural appropriation, its difference from cultural appreciation, and my opinion of these when celebrating the Day of the Dead if you are not of Mexican heritage.

Cultural appropriation is when some aspects of a culture are taken and then used for selfish or disrespectful purposes. Cultural appreciation is when a culture and its aspects are honored in a respectful way, by understanding the context. However, there is a fine line between these two concepts, and people may disagree on where the line exactly lies.

While reading this book and practicing the activities, I recommend taking the following questions into consideration:

YOUR INTENTION: Is your intention clear and do you try to make it clear when sharing it with other people? For example, if you are planning to set up a Day of the Dead altar, is this because you only want to post a picture to your social media or because you genuinely would like to honor your dead loved ones and ancestors? If you post pictures on social media without any context, it may be seen as disrespectful.

ACKNOWLEDGING CONTEXT AND HISTORY: When celebrating *Día de los Muertos* or using one of its symbols, do you understand and acknowledge its meaning and history? For example, if you decide to paint the face of your child as a Catrina, is this because it would look nice as a costume for Halloween, or is it because your child has been afraid of death and telling the history behind the Catrina and characterizing death might be a good way of helping your child overcome the fear? If the image of the Catrina is taken out of context and is used as a "Mexican Halloween costume," some people may find it offensive.

CONGRUENCE: Do you treat Mexican culture and the Day of the Dead with respect, and at the same time, do you treat Mexicans and Latin Americans with respect? For example, if there is a Mexican or Latino community in your area, it might be a good idea to first check if they have any activities open to the general public for *Día de los Muertos* and attend, as well as support the community in any way you are able to.

Having said this, I would like to point out that I see the Day of the Dead as a living and diverse cele-bration. Syncretism is its origin. It developed from the pre-Hispanic world's encounter with European colonialism, and this development continues to unfold across borders and intertwines with other cultures. If you find yourself in the middle of these encounters between cultures, acknowledge the background, the meaning, and the stories behind each symbol. Give respectful credit to the origin of each.

Honoring our dead loved ones and our ancestors is a universal spiritual activity. We all have dead loved ones. We all have ancestors. The ways we honor them may differ in some areas and may be similar in others, but we all may feel the need at some point in our lives to express our grief and our feelings toward the dead.

If the Day of the Dead inspires you to celebrate your loved ones who have passed away, the most important thing is to do so from your heart. When working with the spirit world, it is crucial that what you are doing has meaning to you. If you are motivated to practice some of the activities mentioned in this book, by all means, do so. If some symbols or aspects do not resonate with you, it is more important to

It is crucial that what you are doing ... has meaning to ... you.

find a way to engage with them that does resonate with you. Maybe you do not feel comfortable using the skull as a symbol of death, but you may realize that the picture of a particular animal better symbolizes death for you. Maybe you do not have marigolds available in your area and do not recognize its aroma, but there is another flower that grows during autumn and winter whose aroma helps you remember the past and comforts your heart. Maybe you try setting up a Day of the Dead altar and you do not feel quite connected throughout the process, but perhaps the process later inspires you to take a trip, the same trip around the world that your favorite aunt, who recently died, once took. You decide to honor her life by going to the same places she once saw and that changed her life.

When celebrating a holiday and honoring your ancestors and dead loved ones, do so with respect, and allow it to be an expression of pure love. When celebrating the Day of the Dead, look for the best meaning of what "honoring" means to you, and think of what your dead loved ones would have appreciated. I believe they would still appreciate it. At the end, the way you decide to celebrate them is for them and for you.

INTRODUCTION

Autumn is my favorite season of the year. Since I was a child, I have always looked forward with excitement to the final days of September, when the autumn equinox comes. The rainy season is coming to an end, and, most importantly, some very special guests are about to arrive. It is a strange season, when I feel nostalgic and at the same time cheerful.

In autumn, days start getting shorter and nights longer. The colder weather and the darkness spark thoughts of death, but they are happy thoughts: people who have died recently and how I loved them so much, endings that happened this year and how they changed me, people and situations that are no longer part of my life but that I am deeply grateful for.

During these autumn days, the light looks different, clearer or whiter. The light shines on the trees and the leaves that are changing color. The rays of light between leaves and the sweet aroma on the cold air charm me and make me travel in my thoughts.

I end up thinking about my connections to all-that-is, to Spirit and deity; connections to my present, to the people in my life; connections to my past, to my ancestors and those who have passed away; and connections to my future, those connections that do not exist yet and people who have not arrived in my life yet—possibilities of connections I can feel in the air.

During the first weeks of October, I prepare for a big party that will start at the end of the month. Excited about what is about to happen, I clean the windows, dust the furniture, and sweep the floor. I clear the table and bring out a special tablecloth. I make all the necessary arrangements for my home to be ready and presentable for the guests who are about to arrive. I go to the local market and buy *cempasúchil* flowers, best known as marigolds, a dozen white candles, half a dozen sugar skulls, and *papel picado.* I want the feast to look spectacular. I take a look at the pantry and the bar to see if I have enough of my guests' favorite food and drinks. I want these guests to feel as comfortable and as welcomed as possible.

However, these guests are not average guests: They come once a year for a short period of time. They are very close to me, but at the same time there is a distance between us. And they will come to enjoy the feast in spirit. These guests are special. These guests are dead.

Celebrating the Day of the Dead

El Día de los Muertos, the Day of the Dead, is a celebration dedicated to those dear to us who have passed away. For a few days, we celebrate the lives of those who came before us, we honor them, we welcome them to our homes, and we share our abundance with them. We remember them, and even though the memories come with nostalgia, it is a joyful celebration.

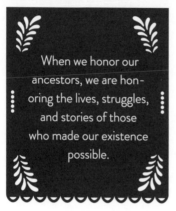

When we honor our ancestors, we are honoring the lives, struggles, and stories of those who made our existence possible.

I was born in Mexico City, and it has always been my hometown. The Day of the Dead has been part of my life since I was a child. My family gets together every year to set up the Day of the Dead altar, just as we do to set up the Christmas tree. We sit at the table and look at the family albums to select the pictures of our beloved ones while telling stories of our relatives and the history of our family, and then we decorate the Day of the Dead altar together.

When I was in elementary school, we were asked every year to follow the teacher across the building to see the huge Day of the Dead altar. We would get in line and observe the long altar, a hall full of flowers, pictures of teachers who had died, and hundreds of sugar skulls, one named for each student from kindergarten through high school. At the end of the path, the founder and director of the school, Miss Meche, would give us a *pan de muerto* and a warm hug one by one.

Honoring our ancestors is an individual, group, and universal activity. When we honor our ancestors, we are honoring the lives, struggles, and stories of those who made our existence possible. As an individual, we are honoring those who came before our parents. As a family, we honor those who created and shaped our group or tribe. And as a community, we honor all those who came before us and built our culture.

By remembering our ancestors and dead loved ones, we may find comfort in our hearts. It also helps us learn about our history and understand our present. By looking for pictures, asking relatives, and investigating, we may find many answers to our questions about why things were the way they were, and why things are the way they are now. We may also find a common origin of all of us. If we look back at our ancestors, our ancestors' ancestors, and further, at some point our ancestors knew each other, and later on, at some point, we all share ancestry.

We celebrate death because death is not the end. Death is a transformation. We celebrate the lives our loved ones lived and we honor them. We celebrate the love we shared.

We celebrate that we met. And we celebrate, as an act of faith, that we will meet again.

How to Use This Book

In this book, I share my personal experience with the Day of the Dead, a brief explanation of its origin, and a glimpse to the diverse activities of the celebration. I talk about the symbol of death around the world and how death is celebrated across the globe. I later share some recommendations on how you can celebrate the Day of the Dead.

Celebrating and honoring your dead loved ones and ancestors is foremost a personal practice and experience. You may find that some of the *actividades* (exercises and activities) align with your personal beliefs and practices, while others may seem quite different from what you are used to. You may be inspired to perform some of the *actividades* exactly as they are written, while you may adapt others to your own way of doing things. This is fine. The most important thing when honoring your ancestors and loved ones is to do and feel it from the heart.

Honoring our ancestors and loves ones is also a universal activity; it does not belong to a particular culture or nationality. We all have people we descended from and most of us know someone who has already passed away. Humanity has honored death and the dead since the beginning of time. The celebrations and symbols of death across different parts of history and across different regions have differences and similarities. In this book, I talk about the Day of the Dead, which is widely diverse on its own.

The Day of the Dead celebration's origin and syncretism are a testament to the encounter between two different worlds, the Mesoamerican and the European. The diversity of the celebration today, found in the unique traditions of each region and indigenous group, is an expression of the history of each region and group. And while more groups of different people meet and engage today across national and international borders, through physical or virtual interactions, the celebration keeps

evolving and in some cases changing, mingling with other celebrations and cultures, creating a new history to tell.

In some urban areas of Mexico, as well as among some Mexican and Latin American populations in other countries, such as the United States, the Day of the Dead and Halloween interact with each other. Some homes or streets may have sugar skulls and candles as *ofrendas*, as well as pumpkins, ghosts, and witches as decorations. Some children may go out trick-or-treating dressed as Catrinas. While some people may not agree with me and find this offensive, I find it understandable, as some families and communities may have multicultural backgrounds, and both celebrations happen around the same time of the year. Also, some of both celebrations' symbols have been integrated into popular culture and have been absorbed into our collective minds through books, television shows, movies, and memes.

Besides the time of the year and the syncretism in their history, we can find other similarities between the Day of the Dead and Halloween. A part of celebrating Halloween is making fun of our deepest and darkest fears. The Day of the Dead invites us to laugh at one of our biggest fears: death. But it is very important to distinguish them from each other, to not call the Day of the Dead "the Mexican Halloween."

Whether you are Mexican, of Mexican descent, Latin American, or of Latin American descent, or none of these, you may still find yourself interested in the Day of the Dead and you may feel inspired to celebrate it. There is a slight and subjective difference between appropriating and appreciating a culture. In my opinion, it depends on the context and individual scenario, especially when it comes to spiritual practices. However, the most important thing to take into consideration is respect: treat the culture respectfully, recognize its origin, and acknowledge the difference and uniqueness when it is mixed with our other personal practices and beliefs.

I hope that, with this book, you feel inspired to celebrate and honor your own ancestors and dead loved ones. I hope this book helps you ponder your own idea of what life and death mean to you and how you deal with this duality. If you feel inspired to celebrate the Day of the Dead and to do some of the activities described in the book, I would consider this a secondary accomplishment.

In some sections of the book, you will read about some flowers, foods, drinks, or symbols that may be hard for you to find in the region where you live or that you may not find relatable to your own path. My intention is to share the meaning of these symbols and for you to find this meaning within your own symbols. The essence of the Day of the Dead is honoring and celebrating those who were, and are, still dear to us, but who have already passed away and sharing with them our abundance and our gratefulness. How each of us celebrates, honors, shares abundance, and expresses gratitude is, at its core, a personal experience.

In the author's note, I shared some notes about how to recognize the difference between cultural appropriation and cultural appreciation. As mentioned before, the key is respect and recognition. However, in order to get to this point, it is important to understand the origin and the context of the celebration, which takes us to our next chapter.

Chapter One

THE HISTORY
OF THE DAY
OF THE DEAD

Nowadays, more than forty indigenous groups in Mexico hold rituals associated with the Day of the Dead. These indigenous celebrations about death mainly take place in territories located in the center-south of Mexico and are shared with non-indigenous populations that live in these areas. Some indigenous populations celebrate for weeks, during the whole month of November, while others just celebrate for a couple of days at the end of October and the start of November.

In some indigenous Mexican communities, especially in regions of the states of Guerrero, Chiapas, and Oaxaca, the Day of the Dead festivity is seen as a transition from a period of time of scarcity to a period of time of abundance. It is a celebration of the harvest, in which people share their abundance with their ancestors, and it is seen as symbolic retribution, as the agricultural cycle would not have been possible without their ancestors' intervention.

The main foundation of the Day of Dead relies on the agricultural cycle and how the people interact with it. The Day of the Dead celebrations are rooted in the customs of the indigenous people of the central and southern areas of Mexico and are linked to the agricultural cycle of maize.

Maize, or corn, has been a very important symbol since pre-Hispanic times. Not only was it the most important basic food and the central axis of the gastronomy and economy, but in the cycle of the grain the people recognized their own cycle, and maize became a mythical symbol, located at the center of the universe. In several pre-Hispanic ancient myths, maize is mentioned as the ingredient the gods used and mixed to create the humans. The world was seen as a field with four sides where the gods were cultivating.

In the cycle of the grain the people recognized their own cycle.

For some indigenous groups, rituals mark each period in order to ensure a successful harvest, and the agricultural year is divided into two complementary halves, the first half of the year being light and dry and the second one being dark and humid. The Day of the Dead is interrelated to its counterpart, the *fiesta de la Santa Cruz*, the Festival of the Crosses (*Visiones de la muerte en el mundo* 2018–2019).

The *fiesta de la Santa Cruz* on May 3, although a Catholic festivity, celebrates the start of the beginning of the rainy season and the start of the sowing of the maize seed. During this celebration, prayers are given to the gods and ancestors, asking their help to ensure fertility and to help the maize grow.

The harvest of the maize starts around mid-October when the rainy season is coming to an end. The Day of the Dead on November 1 and 2 marks the end of the rainy season and the start of the harvest of the maize. The Day of the Dead is considered a celebration in which the first crops are shared with the deceased, who contributed to the development of the maize.

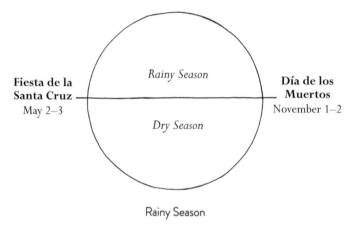

| Fiesta de la Santa Cruz
May 2–3 | *Rainy Season*

Dry Season | Día de los Muertos
November 1–2 |

Rainy Season

The Day of the Dead celebration is diverse. The celebration shares ancient spiritual practices with Catholic traditions. The Spaniards arrival in the central region of Mexico in the sixteenth century brought the Catholic feasts of All Saints' Day and All Souls' Day on November 1 and 2, which matched the dates around when the Nahua celebrated their harvest rituals and festivities, around the end of October and the start of November (Islas 2019).

The celebration has a wide variety of cultural manifestations around the country because of the ethnic and cultural plurality: while in the central-south regions of Mexico the celebrations tend to be more festive, with music and food, in the northern regions they tend to be more mournful (Mata Loera 2020).

The celebration has manifested several artistic creations in music, literature, films, and paintings. It has evolved and has been transformed through the decades.

The roots of the Day of the Dead are pre-Hispanic, but its origin is also Catholic and European; it is a result of an encounter of two worlds and has changed through time, throughout each local population. The celebration is still evolving—it keeps changing while it grows and travels across regions and borders.

Pre-Hispanic Mexico: Mesoamerica (c. 1800 BCE–1521 CE)

Mesoamerica refers to a geographical and historical region where diverse civilizations shared similar characteristics in a time before the Spanish Conquest in what is now Mexico and Central America. Its history is divided into different periods.

The Mesoamerican people considered death to be inherent to life, as part of the constant dual cycle of life and death. For them, it was not how someone lived but the way someone died that defined their destination after dying.

There are representations of the life-death duality from the Preclassic period (c. 1800 BCE–250 CE), and symbols that represent the duality between life and death can be found in ceramic figures, such as two-faced masks or two-headed figures that are missing flesh on one half (Matos Moctezuma 2010, loc. 54 of 177). Signs of elaborate worship of the dead include several burials with offerings such as figures or masks made of clay, which suggests the belief in a life after death (Matos Moctezuma 2014, loc. 170 of 2145).

The Maya (c. 188 BCE–1500 CE) saw the purpose of life as living it the best way possible. They believed in the soul's immortality and that we continued to serve the gods after death. The destiny of their souls was determined by the way of dying. The sacrificed would go to heaven, those who drowned or who had a death related to water would go to the *ceiba* paradise (a realm with a sacred tree in the center), and everyone else would go to the Xibalbá, the Mayan underworld (de la Garza 1999, 40–45).

The Aztecs (c. 1345–1521 CE), also called Mexica, as they referred to themselves, believed that people who had a natural death would go to the Mictlán, the Aztec underworld. The warriors and the women who died during labor would go to a place close to the sun, following its trajectory. The people who drowned or were struck by lightning would go to the Tlalocan, the evergreen paradise. Babies who died from prematurity would go to the Chichihualcuauhco, a wet nurse tree (Matos Moctezuma 2013, 18–20).

Death was also viewed as a maternal womb. Life was conceived and regenerated in the places of death, like the Mictlán. A midwife could say, referring to a baby about to be born, "It is still in the Mictlán" (Johansson 2003, 40–53).

The Aztec civil calendar, Xiuhpōhualli, was composed of eighteen months, each month consisting of twenty days. Months were known as *mētztli*, or *veintenas* (scores). During the eighteen scores throughout the year, there were different festivities dedicated to the dead.

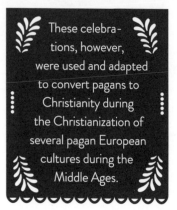

These celebrations, however, were used and adapted to convert pagans to Christianity during the Christianization of several pagan European cultures during the Middle Ages.

Tlaxochimaco, the ninth score of the year (around August 2–24), was the bestowal of flowers, also known as *miccaílhuitl,* "the little feast of the dead." Flowers were the principal symbol of the festivities. People would gather flowers to decorate their temples and offer them to their gods. Flowers and food were also given to the dead (Vela 2014).

The tenth score of the year (around August 25–September 13), *xócotl huetzi,* which means "the falling fruit," was also called *huey miccaílhuitl,* "the great feast of the dead." During this festivity, among other activities, they fasted for three days in honor of the dead and climbed to their roofs and called the dead, facing to the north (Vela 2014).

During the fourteenth score (around November 13–December 2), *quecholli,* which means "precious feather"

arrows were fabricated and dead warriors were honored ("La fecha de hoy y el calendario mexica," n.d.).

The Spanish Conquest:
Influence of the Catholic Celebrations
All Saints' Day and All Souls' Day

The Catholic calendar is driven by the life and death of Jesus and by the memory of those who lived and died following his guidance and example, commemorating saints and martyrs. During the ninth through eleventh centuries, popes and abbots tried to redeem and honor the memory of the martyrs, early Christians who were persecuted.

In France, during the eleventh century, the Abbot of Cluny promoted the celebration of All Saints' Day on November 1 in honor of the Maccabees, a Jewish group recognized as martyrs by the Catholics. This was later accepted by the Roman Church in the thirteenth century, and reinforced by the Council of Trent (1545–63 CE). Churches and monasteries would exhibit the treasures, relics, and remains of the martyrs and saints, and the faithful would visit these temples to venerate the relics and to obtain an indulgence (Conaculta 2006, 46). After the fourteenth-century plagues, November 2 was later designated All Souls' Day for the faithful to offer prayers for them and their loved ones to avoid purgatory and enter heaven (Conaculta 2006, 49).

These celebrations, however, were used and adapted to convert pagans to Christianity during the Christianization of several pagan European cultures during the Middle Ages.

Catholicism came to Mexico with the Spaniards' arrival during the Spanish Conquest (1519–1521) and the Colonial times (1521–1821). The Spanish used violence and forced conversion, destroying symbols of indigenous religions and replacing them with traditional Catholic ones (Frankovich 2019).

The imposition of Christian liturgy after the Spanish conquest led to an adaptation of the calendar of Christian celebrations into the pre-Hispanic agricultural calendars, which were based on astronomical and seasonal observations. These Catholic celebrations were forced and assim-

ilated into the pre-Hispanic existing ones, resulting in syncretism. An example of this syncretism is Our Lady of Guadalupe's worship. Every year around December 12, millions of pilgrims from all around the country go to the basilica on the Hill of Tepeyac in the north of Mexico City, where there used to be a temple dedicated to the Aztec goddess Tonantzin (Noguez 1996, 50–55).

Nowadays, All Saints' Day is celebrated on November 1 to honor the saints and All Souls' Day is celebrated on November 2 to pray to all souls. These religious holidays are indistinctly celebrated with the Day of the Dead by Catholic populations. Some Day of the Dead altars may include Catholic symbols, such as pictures of the Virgin Mary, pictures of Our Lady of Guadalupe, or rosaries.

Early Twentieth-Century Political and Artistic Influence

During the 1930s and 1940s, Mexico had great economic and cultural growth. Along with the artists and intellectuals of the time, the Mexican president Lázaro Cardenas wanted to re-identify what being Mexican meant, focusing more on the pre-Hispanic background. Artists and writers recovered and recreated celebrations and customs and provided a new meaning to them with a national and pre-Hispanic value.

An example of these expressions is the graphic production of José Guadalupe Posada, a political lithographer famous for his death illustrations, the most important being "La Calavera Garbancera," later known as "La Catrina" when it was renamed and painted by Diego Rivera. Other examples include the academic literature of Octavio Paz; the poems written by José Gorostiza, like "Muerte sin Fin" (Death Without End, 1939); the paintings of Diego Rivera, like the mural *Día de Muertos* (1923–1928); and the paintings of Frida Kahlo, like *El difunto Dimas* (1937). In *El laberinto de la soledad* (The Labyrinth of Solitude), Octavio Paz writes,

> *Para el habitante de Nueva York, París o Londres, la muerte es la palabra que jamás pronuncia porque quema los labios. El mexicano, en cambio, la frecuenta, la burla, la acaricia, duerme con ella, la festeja, es uno de sus juguetes favoritos y su amor más permanente.* (Paz 1950, 52)

The word death is not pronounced in New York, in Paris, in London, because it burns the lips. The Mexican, in contrast, is familiar with death, jokes about it, caresses it, sleeps with it, celebrates it; it is one of his favorite toys and his most permanent love.

The Day of the Dead Today

The Day of the Dead is a result of syncretism and of long cultural processes. The Day of the Dead is a product of the encounter of two worlds and different cultures. It is traditionally celebrated on November 1 and November 2, the first dedicated to the souls of the children and the second to the adults. In some regions, it is celebrated for more days or weeks around these dates. In 2008, the United Nations Educational, Scientific, and Cultural Organization (UNESCO) inscribed the Day of the Dead as Intangible Cultural Heritage of Humanity.

The celebration has also been incorporated into modern culture. One example is the video game *Grim Fandango* (1998); the Day of Dead was the main inspiration for the game. Other examples are recent big-production movies that have shown the Day of the Dead or have been based entirely on the celebration. Animated films such as 20th Century Fox's *The Book of Life* (2014), directed by Jorge Gutierrez; Disney/Pixar's *Coco* (2017), directed by Adrian Molina; and Metacube's *Día de Muertos* (2019), also known as *Salma's Big Wish* and directed by Carlos Gutierrez Medrano, have increased the popularity of the festivity around the globe. Some have even reshaped the celebration. In 2016, for example, Mexico City held the first Day of the Dead parade, inspired by a previously released famous James Bond film, *Spectre* (2015), that showed a parade in its opening scene. The now-annual parade did not exist before the movie.

The Day of the Dead is not only a gathering between the dead and the living but also a gathering between the members of the community. Ironically, the Day of the Dead, a celebration of death, is a living tradition. It has changed and evolved through time and still does.

The Diversity of the Day of the Dead

The Day of the Dead is not a single uniform festivity with the same specific activities held across all regions. Although festivities may have similar or common concepts, the Day of the Dead consists of a diversity of celebrations that differ in each local culture.

Common concepts and activities of the Day of the Dead include these:

> **THE *OFRENDA*, OR ALTAR:** A temporary space set for and dedicated to those honored and remembered during the celebration. The *ofrenda* is usually set on a table and consists of pictures of the

deceased with offerings next to them, such as flowers, candles, food, and drinks.

CEMETERY VISITING AND VIGILS: People visit their loved ones' graves, decorate them, and pay their respects through prayers, offerings, music, and lights.

The following regional list illustrates some examples of emblematic and unique Day of the Dead traditions.

Pomuch, North in the State of Campeche (Southeast Mexico)

Every year, the people of the Mayan community of Pomuch exhume the remains of their dead loved ones, clean the bones, and change the cloth that covers them as part of their preparations for the Day of the Dead. The ritual is known as *Choo Ba'ak* (Mayan, meaning "cleaning of bones"). Family members visit the graveyard and extract the bones of their dead loved ones. They open the wooden box and gently clean the bones with a brush, starting with the small bones and then moving on to bigger bones. While they clean, they speak to the loved one. As an offering, they also change the white cloth with colorful embroidery of flowers and crosses that will cover the remains for a year. It is a yearly tradition but can only be done if three years have passed since the person died. It is an expression of love and respect. It is said that if they do not clean the bones, the spirit will be upset.

Totonacapan Region, North in the States of Veracruz and Puebla (East Mexico)

The Totonac people celebrate *Ninin*, their festivity of the Day of the Dead, for forty-two days. The celebration is divided in two parts: the first is dedicated to those who had violent, accidental, or drowning deaths; the second to those who had a natural death. The first one starts on October 18, the feast of Saint Luke, a saint who is said to have replaced their god of thunder. The bells of the churches ring, guiding the souls, and the families gather to start preparing the food for their offerings. The sec-

A little altar is set outside the house, dedicated to the souls of the orphans

ond part starts at noon of October 31, dedicated to the souls of the children. A little altar is set outside the house, dedicated to the souls of the orphans. At noon on November 1 they receive the souls of the adults. On November 2 they visit the graves of their loved ones with music and songs of praise. On November 8 and 9, during the *aktumajat* (the eighth day after All Saints' Day), they say goodbye to their dead loved ones with prayers. On November 30 the souls of the dead leave.

San Andrés Mixquic, Southeast Mexico City (Valley of Mexico)

In San Andrés Mixquic, in southeast Mexico City, the celebration begins on the sunset of November 1. A path made of flowers guides the entrance of the town to the cemetery. Candles are lit and music is played by *mariachis*. They hold a contest for skulls made of cardboard. They stage a funeral procession in which they ask people for financial help for the funeral, the people yell satirical and funny phrases to the "dead," and then the dead jumps and runs through the crowds along with laughs, jokes, and music. The next day's celebration is solemn, with the *alumbrada* ("the lit [vigil]"), during which people go to the cemetery with flowers, candles, and incense—everything looks magically lit up. They pray to the dead until the ringing of bells announces the souls have returned to the Mictlán.

Huasteca Region, South in the State of Tamaulipas, North Veracruz, East San Luis Potosi, North Hidalgo, North Puebla, and North Queretaro (East Mexico)

The Huastec people call their Day of the Dead celebrations *Xantolo*, which comes from the Latin word *sanctorum* ("holy"). Their celebrations start on September 29 with the feast of Saint Michael, when they start buying the items for their altar. On October 18, the feast of Saint Luke, they go to the graveyards to clean the graves. The altar is set at the homes from October 31 to November 8. The celebration ends on November 30 with Saint Andrew's feast. The celebrations include dances related to the harvest of the maize and masks ("Xantolo Xalapa 2019, tradición e identidad," 2020).

State of Yucatan, Southeast Mexico

The Yucatecans and Maya celebrate *Hanal Pixán,* which means "food for the souls." The first day, October 31, is dedicated to the souls of the children. November 1 is dedicated to the dead adults. November 2 is dedicated to all souls. The traditional and regional food plays a big part in the celebration, including the *mucbipollo*, or *pib*, a big *tamale* made of flour and butter with chicken or pork meat, prepared with tomato and chili and cooked in a ground oven. Some make a ritual to thank the earth before preparing the pit. The *pib* is eaten after prayers are made and it is offered to the dead.

Isthmus of Tehantepec, States of Veracruz, Oaxaca, Chiapas, and Tabasco (South Mexico)

The Zapotec people celebrate *Xandu'*, which comes from the Spanish word *santo* (saint). It is celebrated on October 30 and 31. They believe that the cold wind is the sign that souls are arriving. They believe the soul's journey to the other side takes three months, so they only celebrate people who have died more than three months before. The ones who recently died are celebrated next year. It is not customary to visit graves, and people mainly celebrate with their altars made at their homes. They have two types of altars. The first is called *biguié* or *biyé,* a wooden frame that marks each cardinal point and the center with flowers, banana leaves, and fruits. The second is an altar made of seven levels ("Xandu', Día de Muertos zapoteco del Istmo de Tehuantepec," 2018).

CONSEJO (TIP)

When celebrating *Día de los Muertos* and inviting your dead loved one to your altar, you may wonder what would happen if different people or different households invite the same spirit to their altars. Whom would the spirit visit?

I would like to explain this from my personal point of view. We sometimes think of spirits as being just like us but without flesh. However, spirits are not bound to the same rules of time and space as we are. When we pray to deities or spiritual beings, like angels, several different people may be praying to the same deity or spiritual being at the same time, and that deity or being may be present or manifesting with each one. Similarly, when we call or think of our dead loved one, that spirit may be with us and at the same time with another person who is thinking of the same spirit.

Think about it this way. When someone we love dies, they remain in our hearts. Our love for them does not go away. That love links us to that spirit. The Day of the Dead is often romantically described as spirits visiting us. But the way I see it is that they never left. During the time of the celebration, the veil between the dead and the living is thinner, so we perceive them closer for a brief time. Two different people or households may have the same loved one in their hearts, and they both are able to be closer with the loved one at the same time during the Day of the Dead celebration.

For example, my mom and I do not live together. During *Día de los Muertos*, we both include my maternal grandmother in our altars. We both loved her deeply. We both still think of her, miss her, and love her. We both feel her presence during the celebration at our homes, and she visits me and my mother because she is in both of our hearts.

Costa Chica of the Guerrero Region, South in the State of Guerrero (South Mexico)

The Afromexican people of the Costa Chica of Guerrero celebrate the Day of the Dead with the *danza de los diablos* ("dance of the devils"). The origin of this dance comes from the Colonial times (1521–1810): it was a ritual dedicated to the African god Ruja as a petition to be liberated from slavery ("La Danza de los Diablos; patrimonio afromexicano en la Costa Chica de Guerrero," 2019). However, "no mention" of modern cults of Ruja is found today (Vaughn 2001, 17). The dance is performed by a group of a dozen people wearing masks, beards, and fringes made of horsehair and long rags. The main characters of the dance are the *diablo mayor* ("great devil") and the *minga*. Some believe the diablos represent the spirits of the dead, while others believe they represent intermediaries between life and death. The music played is called *chilena,* introduced to the region by Chilean sailors in the nineteenth century (Vaughn 2001, 17).

Ocotepec, North of Cuernavaca, State of Morelos (Center-South of Mexico)

The people of the town of Ocotepec, in the state of Morelos, have a very special way of celebrating the Day of the Dead and when creating their altar, they simulate a corpse. On a table, they recreate the body of the deceased dressed in the clothes and shoes the deceased used to wear. They place a sugar skull as a head and offerings, food, and drinks around the body. When the deceased has recently died, it is called an *ofrenda nueva* ("new ofrenda"), and neighbors and friend of the deceased visit the *ofrenda*. The hosts give food and drinks to the visitors as appreciation, and the visitors have to bring a candle to light the path of the deceased on his way back home ("Ocotepec celebrará Día de Muertos, tradición reconocida por la UNESCO," 2014).

Death as Part of Life

The Mesoamerican people used to see death as part of life. The way people died defined the destiny of their souls after death. The Spaniards' arrival and the conversion to Christianity caused an adaptation of beliefs and rituals, resulting in syncretism. Political and artistic movements in the twentieth century recovered and revived pre-Hispanic and national values, including the way Mexicans relate to death. The celebration has been integrated into pop culture, especially into recent famous movies.

Nowadays, the Day of the Dead, declared an Intangible Cultural Heritage of Humanity by the United Nations, is mainly celebrated on November 1 and November 2, interrelated with the Catholic religious holidays of All Saints' Day and All Souls' Day.

The history of the Day of the Dead is diverse, as are the variety of its rituals and traditions in different regions and populations. However, the common base of the Day of the Dead celebration in indigenous groups is the agricultural cycle: when the rainy season is coming to an end, the people share the harvest and abundance with their dead loved ones and express their gratitude to them.

We do not only celebrate the dead, but we also celebrate with them and because of them. We thank them for the abundance we have in our lives, whether it is physical abundance or spiritual abundance. They may have been direct or indirect contributors to that abundance. We are today because of what they once were. We have what we own today because of what once they gave to us.

Everything has a cycle. There are times for sowing as there are times for harvesting; there are times for persisting as there are times for celebrating; there are times to welcome as there are times to let go. Our existence has also a cycle, life, and death. Death is not the end, as it is the counterpart of life; death follows life, but it is followed by life as well. Death is a transformation.

chapter one

Chapter Two
DEATH

Since the beginning of time, humanity has been amazed by the forces of nature and by the forces of life. We have observed the nature around us—the skies, the earth, the elements—and have tried to explain what happens with stories and names. Names and stories vary within each culture and time; however, all around the world each culture has generated its own cosmology and myths,

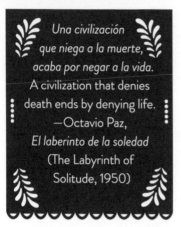

> *Una civilización que niega a la muerte, acaba por negar a la vida.*
> A civilization that denies death ends by denying life.
> —Octavio Paz,
> *El laberinto de la soledad*
> (The Labyrinth of Solitude, 1950)

and names were given to these forces, recognizing them as spirits, deities, gods, or goddesses.

There are countless deities associated with death and the underworld around the world. Some commonly known ones are the ancient Egyptian god Anubis, the Greek god Hades, the Nordic goddess Hel, and the Celtic goddess the Morrigan.

In *El laberinto de la soledad*, Octavio Paz writes,

> *Una civilización que niega a la muerte, acaba por negar a la vida.* (Paz 1950, 63)

A civilization that denies death ends by denying life.

Pre-Hispanic Deities of Death and the Underworld

Different names and myths for these forces can be found in the diverse Mesoamerican cultures. Some names and myths concur across cultures and regions; some are similar, while others are very different. Here are some pre-Hispanic forces or deities associated with death and the underworld.

Mictlantecuhtli and Mictecacihuatl: Aztec, Central Mexico

The couple Mictlantecuhtli and Mictecacihuatl are the rulers of the Mictlán, the underworld. They are usually represented as disembodied or as skeletons. Souls travel through the nine stages of the Mictlán and go through several trials until finding rest with them.

Coatlicue: Aztec, Central Mexico

Coatlicue is the great Aztec earth goddess, the mother of gods. Her name means "Serpent Skirt" because of the skirt full of snakes she wears. She wears human skulls, hands, and hearts on her breast. She is a major deity of life, death, and fertility. This dualistic concept of the earth goddess represents the idea that life contains the seed of death.

Coyolxauhqui: Aztec, Central Mexico

Coyolxauhqui, "She of the Bells Painted on Her Face," is the Aztec goddess of the moon, daughter of the earth goddess Coatlicue, and sister of the sun god Huitzilopochtli. Her myth explains the phases of the moon and how the moon dies to allow the birth of the sun, representing the cycle of life and death.

Coatlicue (the earth) was sweeping her temple hill Coatepec, the serpent hill, when she saw that some feathers fell from the sky. She picked them up and placed them in her womb. When she finished sweeping, she searched for the feathers, but she couldn't find them. She realized she was pregnant. This event offended her children: her daughter Coyolxauhqui (the moon) and her sons the *centzonhuitznahuas* (the southern stars). Coyolxauhqui convinced her brothers to kill their mother. Cuahuitlicac, one of the southern stars, warned their mother. However, inside the womb, Huitzilopochtli (the sun) heard the warning and told Coatlicue not to worry. Huitzilopochtli was born dressed as a warrior and armed with a serpent of fire, the *xiuhcoatl* (the sun's ray). With the *xiuhcoatl*, Huitzilopochtli beheaded Coyolxauhqui, who fell, shattered, down the hill. The *centzonhuitznahuas* tried to run away, terrified. But Huitzilopochtli caught them, destroying some of them and banishing the others.

Cihuacóatl: Aztec, Central Mexico

Cihuacóatl means "Serpent Woman." She is the goddess of the women who died in childbirth. She is made of stone and has large and angry teeth. She has long and heavy hair and is dressed all in white.

Xolotl: Aztec, Central Mexico

Xolotl is the twin brother of Quetzalcóatl. Quetzalcóatl announces the sunrise, and Xolotl the sunset, giving the sun company during its continuous journey through the land of the dead. Being a twin-brother deity, Xolotl is associated with duality, darkness, and the underworld. He is considered to be the patron of witches. He is usually represented as a dog.

Tlaltecuhtli: Aztec, Central Mexico

Tlaltecuhtli is a goddess of the earth who, in a birthing position, devours the body of the deceased through a vagina with huge teeth and fangs, representing the dead being eaten by the earth. Later, the individual would go through the womb, as a rite of passage, until they were released through birth to their journey and determined destiny. She is a dual deity of life and death, of devouring-birthing (Matos Moctezuma 2013, 18–22).

Ah Puch: Maya, Southeastern Mexico and Central America

Ah Puch is an androgynous deity of the dead and the underworld, represented with a skeletal body and signs of decomposition. Ah Puch, meaning "the Disembodied One," is also known with the names Kisin ("the Flatulent One"), Yum Kimil ("the Lord of Death"), or Kimi ("Death").

Pitao Pezeelao and Xonaxi Queculla: Zapotec Culture, Oaxaca

God and goddess of death and the underworld, Pitao Pezeelao and Xonaxi Queculla are a couple, and both gods were the principal deities in the region before the Spanish conquest. Owls are their messengers, and turkeys were given to them as offerings. They are worshipped for success in battle and help during pandemics.

Modern Representations of Death

La Llorona

La Llorona, "the Weeping Woman," is a famous Mexican legend of the spirit of a woman who is said to appear in the streets of Mexico City and to cry for her children "*¡Ay, mis hijos!*" (Oh, my children!)

It is said that the legend comes from Colonial times, when an indigenous woman fell in love with a Spanish nobleman, and they had children together. He later left her for a Spanish woman of his own social level, and she lost her mind, slaying her children. She now wanders the streets, dressed in white, crying for her children.

Some see la Llorona's origin as pre-Hispanic, coming from the myth of the mother goddesses Tonantzin, Cihuacoatl, and Coatlicue.

La Santa Muerte

La Santa Muerte, also known as Santísima Muerte, Hermana Blanca ("White Sister"), Santa Niña ("Saint Girl"), Señora ("Lady"), Mi Amor ("My Love"), Magnífica ("Magnificent"), Madrina ("Godmother"), la Doña ("the Lady/the Madam"). She is the Mexican folk saint of death. She is seen by devotees as a protector and as a lady of justice. It is said she is the patroness of those who are in constant danger, but she protects anyone who asks for her protection. She is mainly celebrated on August 15 and on November 2.

She is represented by a human skeleton wearing a robe and a cloak, expressing pureness. She has a halo above her skull, representing divinity. She often carries a scale, representing justice; a scythe, representing time and the termination of life; a terrestrial globe, representing the fragility of the world; and sometimes an owl, an hourglass, a book, or a dagger. She is represented standing up, holding one of the mentioned items or with her arms open, or sitting down on a throne or a globe (Perdigón Castañeda 2008, 77–78).

While some people are afraid of her image, her devotees describe her often as a white, female figure who irradiates light, sweetness, and peace. She is not seen as either good or evil; she is seen as an intermediary. Some say that if you do not comply with what you promised to her in exchange for a favor, she will take the life of a loved one. However, others do not agree with this and believe the worship should come from a place of love and faith, and not from fear (Perdigón Castañeda 2008, 85).

The roots of her worship are unclear. Some see her as a rebirth of Mictecacihuatl, the Aztec Lady of Death and the Underworld. Others see her origin in the European introduction of the Grim Reaper, a medieval skeletal figure with a scythe and a robe that originated with the Black Death during the fourteenth century.

The Catholic Church has condemned the worship of la Santa Muerte, but her worship keeps growing, and its prayers and rituals mimic Catholicism's. The media and the Catholic Church have spread a negative image of la Santa Muerte, associating her with evil, black magic, and criminal activity. Because of this, a lot of people have a negative bias against her and her worshipers.

The worship of la Santa Muerte used to be hidden decades ago, as devotees were afraid of being attacked. Nowadays, it is more common to see the figure of la Santa Muerte as a pendant, on street art, and in public altars.

Our Relationship with Death

Death is part of everything because everything has a cycle. Death and life have an intimate relationship of opposite sides that continuously attract each other. To think about how we are currently living makes us think about how we are going to die, and to think about how we are going to die makes us think about how we are living today. We like to think that the living will remember us after we die, and we think of those who are already gone.

Death is also fair and unbiased. She will one day come for each one of us regardless of our nationality, religion, gender, sexual orientation, or economic status. No one can escape from it. She makes us all equal—we are all going to die someday.

Death is a phase of the cycle of life. Death is unavoidable; no one can escape it. Death is impartial; it does not discriminate. Death is unpredictable; we cannot know when it will exactly happen. Death is contradictory; it is an end that instantly comes but has been present among us since we took our first breath. Death is diverse; it is seen and celebrated differently across the world.

Death is experienced and celebrated all across the world and differently by each culture. Humanity has always had special rituals and activities to say goodbye to and to remember the deceased. There are different views and words all around the globe regarding death.

In Mexico we have a very unique view of death. We play with her. We laugh with her. We make fun of her. We dress her. We name her. We write about her. We sing about her. We paint her. We made a national symbol out of her. And once a year we celebrate her.

During the Day of the Dead, we remember those close to us who have died. The celebration spreads all around the country and across both of our borders. It is celebrated by the masses without distinction of social, cultural, or economic backgrounds. It is celebrated by all different types of people, without regard to age or beliefs.

In Mexico we personalize Death. We kid about her, we use satire with her, we create a character out of her, we talk with her, we honor her, and we name her.

There are hundreds of ways Mexicans refer to death. These colloquialisms or local references to death are a way of using humor around a sensitive subject and making fun of it and are usually used in the feminine. Some examples of these names include the following:

- La Calva, "the Bald One"
- La Flaca, "the Skinny One"
- La Blanca, "the White One"
- La Cabezona, "the Big-Headed One"
- Doña Huesos, "Mrs. Bones"
- La Cruel, "the Cruel One"
- La Llorona, "the Weeping One"

- La Dientuda, "the One with Big Teeth"

- La Pálida, "the Pallid One"

- La Apestosa, "the Stinky One"

- La Triste, "the Sad One"

- La Güera, "the Blonde One"

- La Huesuda, "the Bony One"

- La Liberadora, "the Liberator"

These names come up in normal conversations. For example, someone could say, "*La Flaca se lo llevó* (The Skinny One took him)," and we would understand what the person means: he died, or death took him.

We also have sayings or colloquial phrases that we use as metaphors to refer to as synonyms of "dying" or "to die." For example, "*Estiró la pata*" (He/She stretched the leg) refers to the how the body gets rigid when dying. Other examples are "*Se lo llevó la Flaca al baile*" (The Skinny One took him to the ball), "*Colgó los tenis*" (He/She hung the sneakers), and "*Colgó los guantes*" (He/She hung the gloves), meaning that the person died and will no longer wear them.

One popular saying is "*Chupó faros*." *Chupar* means "to suck," and *Faros* is an old Mexican brand of cigarettes. It is said that the phrase comes from the Mexican Revolution (1910–1917) or from the Cristero War (1926–1929): when soldiers were going to be shot, they were allowed to smoke a cigarette as a last wish. Some of these sayings, including *chupar faros*, are used not only to refer to "to die" but also as synonyms for when something is finished or runs out. For example:

"What happened to the cookies? The box is empty."

"*Chupó faros.*"

Death is part of Mexican culture, so it is also part of our language. By comparing death to something else or replacing it with another concept, we understand it better. When we associate death with other situations, we create a close relationship with it.

These names and sayings that we use in informal speaking may help us better understand why the Day of the Dead is not just an act of grief. It does not come out of sadness, although at some moments of the celebration we may be sad; we play with death, we celebrate her, and we celebrate with her by laughing with her.

Death is part of Mexican culture, so it is also part of our language.

• ACTIVIDAD 1 •
Name Death

When we are afraid of something, it sometimes helps to make fun of it. Laughing dissolves and wards the fear off. If you are scared of death, think of a funny way to refer to it that describes the reason you are afraid of it. For example, one thing I do not like about death is that we never know when it will happen and that there can never be an appropriate time for someone to die. It is something you cannot plan or fully be prepared for. So I would describe death as an awkward visitor that arrives at an unfortunate time: la Inoportuna ("the Untimely One").

If you cannot think of something you are afraid of, you can try to think of something you could use to describe death. For example, I sometimes see death as insensitive because she does not care about others' feelings when it is time for her to take someone with her, and also the body gets cold when someone dies, so I would name death la Fría ("the Cold One").

Think about how you feel about death. Do you feel fear? Do you avoid the topic? Does it make you sad? Does it make you nostalgic? What makes you feel this way? Is it the way you have lived? Is it the way you have not been able to live yet? Is it because you have lost someone you cared a lot for? How would you describe that feeling, using an adjective? If death were a character in a funny movie, how would you describe her?

• ACTIVIDAD 2 •
Draw Death

Now that you have created a character for death with a concept and words, try picturing how she would look. Is she dressed in formal clothes, or is she poorly dressed? Is she wearing modern or old-fashioned clothes?

Grab a piece of paper and colored pencils. Start by drawing a skeleton, the skull and the bones for each part of the body. Later, add clothing and items to it. For example, you can add a hipster beard and a mobile phone to her right hand because you picture death as always up-to-date, or maybe you can add sunglasses and a hoodie because you consider her to work always hidden and incognito.

You don't have to be a great artist to do this. It does not matter how good you consider your drawing skills to be. The important thing is to have fun and have a laugh. You can also use a drawing mobile app or software if you feel more comfortable.

Laugh with death and let the fear go away!

My Relationship with Death

The Day of the Dead has been my favorite celebration since I was a child, and I believe it has been so because I have a special relationship with death. Death is a sensitive subject for many people—it sparks fear, sadness, or anger. And although I may feel fearful, sad, or angry when it's time to say goodbye, I do not see death as a threat of an end or as a separation. I see it as a celebration and as a transformation. I see, feel, and think of death as a loving process of our overall existence.

I inherited this special relationship I have with death from my father's side of the family. My grandmother was a gifted woman who could feel when someone was about to die. My father, a few cousins, and I feel this too. I was thirteen years old when I experienced it for the first time. I was in a movie theater with a friend, and out of the blue I suddenly felt a great sadness in my heart and a heavy sensation on my shoulders. My friend noticed I was anxious. We left the movie theater and walked for a couple of hours while I tried to calm down. A few hours later, I received a phone call from my father, who told me an uncle had just died. I realized that what I had just felt was probably because of the news, and just as I received the news, the sensation went away and I felt relieved. I felt a peaceful sensation, as in everything was now fine.

These relatives and I also dream of the dead often. The first dream I can remember is when I was nine years old and my favorite aunt died. A couple of weeks after she passed away, I had a dream in which she visited me and hugged me. I remembered feeling her bones and screaming in fear, and she told me to not be afraid, that death was a normal part of our lives, that it had nine stages and she was going through them. I looked around and we were in a garden surrounded by stone walls made of skulls. She said to me she did not want me to be sad, that she was visiting me because she wanted me to know that she was okay.

My grandmother Yolanda is a common character in my dreams. In a dream, three years ago, she was in the kitchen, and she warned me that everything was unstable and that there was going to be a lot of movement, but that I was going to be okay. Three days later we had a very strong earthquake in Mexico City. Two years ago I dreamed that she sat on my bed and put her hands on my hand. She only said, "It's okay. It's time to let go." The next day my relationship with my now ex-husband ended.

A few months ago, one of my cousins had a dream in which she visited my father's house. My father was cooking and our ancestors were sitting at the table. My cousin tried to taste the food that my father was cooking and putting on the table, but our ancestors told her she could not eat from this feast, that it was not her time to take from the table of the dead. The next day, she called my father and told him her dream. My father was surprised—he had the exact same dream that night. In his dream, he was cooking and my cousin visited his house. While he was in the kitchen, he heard she tried to taste the food and that our ancestors told her not to.

Every New Year's Eve, after making a toast for the New Year and hugging each other, we also make a toast for those who are not with us anymore.

My family also talks about the dead often, and we integrate them into our lives. Every New Year's Eve, for instance, after making a toast for the New Year and hugging each other, we also make a toast for those who are not with us anymore. I remember being a child and scared because after this toast, a chair would suddenly fall down or a door would be shut out of the blue. My family would only laugh and raise their glass again.

Although most of my family is Catholic and I was raised like one, my parents always encouraged me to explore my spirituality. They gave me books about different spiritual subjects and a tarot card deck. They discussed spiritual and magical topics with me and my siblings and asked us how we felt and what we thought. I was very lucky to be raised in a supportive and open-minded environment, and when I was thirteen years old, I found my spiritual path: Wicca. I recognized my path in Wicca because I have always had a lot of curiosity toward magic. I had always felt closer to the divine feminine and always found it very interesting that everything has a cycle. Earth goes through seasons and is renewed, and the cycle starts again. The moon has its phases: it goes through the new moon and grows until the full moon, then fades away until it is dark and starts again. The cycle of life and death is part of all of our existence.

Celebrations of Death around the World

Cultures around the world have identified death differently. Ideas of death are manifested in funerary rites and celebrations to honor the dead to establish a channel of communication between the dead and the living. Although some people see death as the end, many cultures see it as a transformative process, the beginning of another phase.

In ancient Egypt, for example, people believed in life after death. Death was seen as a state of transition where the spiritual essences faced challenges and trials in their journey through the underworld, just like the sun. As the sun "dies" through the West, and is reborn through the East, it was believed people could be reborn.

The Day of the Dead, celebrated mainly in Mexico and Latin America, is not the only celebration in the world associated with death. Here are some examples of other celebrations of death:

Qingming Festival: China and South East Asia

The Qingming Festival, also known as Tomb-Sweeping Day, is one of the public holidays in China and is more than 2,500 years old. It is celebrated between April 4 and 6. The name means *clear* and *bright* because of the weather during this time. When the warmth and rain increases, it is a time for ploughing and sowing. During this festivity, they visit their ancestors' tombs, clean and clear the tombs, offer their ancestors food and flowers. They burn incense and money as an offering and to ask for prosperity. They eat cold food, an event called the Hanshi Festival, and among other activities, they fly kites, attaching lanterns to them.

Památka Zesnulých or Dušičky: Czech Republic

Officially known as *Památka Zesnulých* ("a remembrance of those who have passed") and also known as *Dušičky* ("little souls") or *Všech Svatých* ("of all saints"), this tradition is celebrated on November 2. It is a quiet celebration during which people visit their loved ones' tombs, lay flowers, and light candles. The candles guide the souls during their journey, and the flowers represent life after death. Its origin is linked to pagan Celtic roots.

Obon: Japan

Obon is one of Japan's most popular holidays. It is a Buddhist celebration that originated in the seventh century and is observed around mid-July or mid-August, depending on if the region uses the Gregorian or lunar calendar for the date. It is believed that during Obon, the ancestors' spirits come back to visit their relatives. Although customs vary in each region, offerings are made at house altars and temples, and lanterns are hung outside houses to guide the spirits. They perform dances, called *Bon odori*, to welcome their ancestors. At the end of the festivity, floating lanterns are put into the river in the direction of the ocean, to guide their ancestors to the other side.

Jesa: Korea

Jesa is a Korean memorial ceremony held each year on the death anniversary of a relative, involving a large family gathering with food and drinks, where the family pays respects to their deceased. In the ceremony, they evoke the spirit of the deceased, asking the spirit to join them and explaining the food on the table is for the spirit. They insert a pair of chopsticks into the center of a bowl of rice, as a gesture that the food is offered to the spirit. A photograph of the deceased is placed in the center of the table with a piece of paper with the deceased's name. The piece of paper is burned at the end of the ceremony, indicating to the spirit that it is time to depart (Alper 2016).

Pchum Ben: Cambodia

During *Pchum Ben*, celebrated in October, Cambodians show respect to their ancestors. *Pchum* means "to meet together" and *Ben* means "to collect" or "to mold the rice into portions." It is believed that during this time, spirits come to receive offerings from their relatives. When the living offer food to the spirits, the spirits bless the living.

Awuru Odo: Nigeria

Awuru Odo is celebrated every two years between September and November until April by the Igbo people of Nigeria. The *Odo* are the spirits of the dead, and it is believed they come to visit their families. A big theatrical and ritual performance is made before the spirits' departure, in which participants represent the *Odo* with masks and reenact the story of the spirits visiting and then leaving.

Yizkor: Jewish Memorial Service

Yizkor, which means "remember," is a Jewish memorial service dedicated to the deceased in which loved ones who have died are remembered and prayers are made to them. It is recited four times a year, during Yom Kippur, Shemini Atzeret (the eighth day of Sukkot), Pesach (the last day of Passover), and Shavuot.

Samhain: Death in Modern Paganism

Modern Paganism consists of spiritual and religious traditions such as Wicca, Witchcraft, Druidry, Heathenry, Asatru, and many others. The origins can be traced to twentieth-century England, where traditions like Wicca arose as an effect of the occult movements of the nineteenth century.

Each Pagan tradition and group has its own beliefs and practices. However, modern Pagans generally honor nature and celebrate the cycles of seasons of the earth and phases of the moon, recognizing the cycle of life and death in all the cycles of nature and in our own lives. Pagans usually see death as the beginning of the next phase and usually believe in the afterlife, in some Wiccan traditions called "the Summerland." In many traditions within the Pagan community, blood ancestors are recognized, honored, and remembered along with spiritual ancestors (mentors and tradition leaders) and ancestors of the land.

Many modern Pagan traditions, especially Wicca and Witchcraft, celebrate Samhain on October 31. The Celtic feast of Samhain marks the end of summer and the beginning of winter. It signals the end of the light and warm half of the year and the start of the cold and dark half. It is considered to be the beginning of the year and when the veil between the worlds is thinner. It is a time for magic and divination: a time

I see close similarities ... between Samhain ... and the Day of the Dead.

of communion with the spirits of the dead; a time to call the ancestors, who might have messages or warnings for the year to come; and a time of feast, as the cereal harvest have been completed at this time. The Christian All Souls' Day was used to replace this Celtic pagan holiday. Halloween was developed from this Celtic celebration.

I see close similarities between Samhain and the Day of the Dead, as both are linked to the change of the seasons, to the harvest and feast, and to honoring the dead and the ancestors.

A Worldwide Relationship with Death

Humanity has always embodied the forces of nature, including death. When seeing the powers of nature, we name those powers in an attempt to interact with them. Death has been represented in deities in many cultures across time and continues to be. We personify death in an attempt to lose our fear of it and make fun of it. We name death because it is easier for us to process what we can name and visualize.

Death is widely celebrated around the globe, and there are many traditions dedicated to the dead in different religions and cultures. One of these celebrations is the Day of the Dead, whose main ritual expression is the *ofrenda*, or altar.

Chapter Three
THE DAY OF
THE DEAD ALTAR

The word "altar" comes from the Latin *altus*, which means "high." An altar is a sacred space dedicated to spiritual practices such as rituals or prayers, and it is usually placed on a raised structure (for example, a table).

An altar consists of the structure and of the items representing sacred symbols. Some altars are for permanent use, like for constant spiritual practices of an individual, while others are temporary, like for a specific ritual or festivity. Some are personal, built at home, while others are for the community, like the altars in temples and churches.

The Day of the Dead altar, also known as the *ofrenda* ("offering"), is the center of the celebration. It functions as a sacred place in your home dedicated to the spirits of the dead. The *ofrenda* is a temporary gathering point between the dead and the living where offerings are placed for the ancestors. It is a place of thought, prayer, and remembrance.

The altars are mainly set up inside homes. However, there are also altars created for the general public in cemeteries. They are also created by museums, schools, universities, government offices, and hospitals; these altars usually have a dedicated theme. For example, a hospital's altar may include famous deceased doctors, or a library's altar may include famous deceased writers.

On September 19, 2017, a strong earthquake shook Mexico City and other parts of the country. A month later, in October, several ofrendas were set outside some of the collapsed buildings, dedicated to the deceased victims of the earthquake. In the south of the city, an altar was created in front of the collapsed building of Enrique

Rébsamen School, where nineteen children died. Besides flowers and candles, the altar included juice boxes and toys as an offering for the children. These altars, set on sidewalks, below trees, on streets, and on walls, were not organized by a specific entity or organization; it was a collective effort. Neighbors, relatives of the victims, and others in the community participated.

The Day of the Dead altars are representations of the universe, and within this context they can have a number of different levels, representing the connection of the under-world with the celestial sphere. Although they are commonly set on the same level—or even in some cultures it is set over a mat on the floor—some are set up with different levels. A two-level altar represents the division between the earth and the sky. A three-level altar represents the sky, the earth, and the underworld. An altar of seven to nine levels represents the different levels the soul has to go through before reaching peaceful rest.

I usually set my own altar in only one level, as it is easier to set and maintain and less risky (as you would not like something to fall down), and you can differentiate the individual representations on one level.

The Day of the Dead altar can be slowly set in late October, some days before the Day of the Dead celebrations. Traditionally, the altar is set on the night of October 30 or on November 1, for it to be ready for the arrival of the deceased on November 1 and 2. The setting consists of first gathering all the items of the altar, then inviting your loved ones who have passed away, and guiding them to the altar.

During the festivity, the dead and the ancestors are welcomed at the altar, where food and water are provided to them so they can recover after their travel. At the altar, descendants talk to them and think of them, recalling memories of them in their honor.

After the festivity, the altar is dismantled. It is not left out all year. The *ofrenda* is like setting a table for a fancy feast, where guests come, enjoy, and then leave. After they leave, you clean up and store what you can.

The Day of the Dead altar consists of different items or representations, and each of them will be later explained. If you want to create your own Day of the Dead altar, take into consideration that you will need the following:

- Table or raised surface
- Water

- Cup(s) for the water
- Food and drinks
- *Calaveras* (skulls)
- Incense or copal
- Incense holder
- Flowers

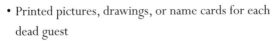

- Printed pictures, drawings, or name cards for each dead guest
- Personal and special objects of the guests, such as toys
- *Pan de muerto* (bread of the dead)
- *Papel picado* (colored cut paper) or colorful table-cloths or paper
- Salt
- Bowl for the salt
- White candles: 1 small for each guest and 2 to 3 larger ones
- Matches or a lighter
- Any religious or spiritual figures or symbols you would like to include

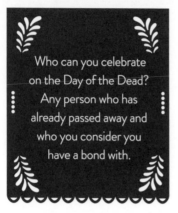

Who can you celebrate on the Day of the Dead? Any person who has already passed away and who you consider you have a bond with.

Hosting the Day of the Dead celebration is similar to hosting a special party. For this party, as for any other one, you will need to first prepare for it. For example, you will make a guest list, including the people invited and the people to whom the celebration is dedicated; the difference is that, on this occasion, the guests are dead. Select a place for the party, the part of your home you will host the party in; on this occasion, the guests are non-physical, so the place consists of a surface where symbols will represent both the guests and the party itself. Gather offerings and related elements and prepare the altar. Display signs to guide the guests to the party and set out representations of the guests and food and drinks that will be given to the guests. Also set out decorations and gifts.

The main part of the celebration consists of guiding your dead loved ones to your home, welcoming them to the altar, making a feast for them, giving them offerings, talking to them and thinking of them, and honoring them.

The end of the celebration consists basically of saying goodbye to the guests, wishing them a good return, and dismantling the altar.

Preparing Your Day of the Dead Altar
A List of the Guests:
Dead Loved Ones and Ancestors

The most important thing at a party is the guest list. The first step is to create a list with the names of all the dead loved ones you are going to include in your Day of the Dead altar and celebrations. The list will function as a guide for you to know how many items you will need total, and later when inviting them to the celebration, you can use it to call them all one by one.

Who can you celebrate on the Day of the Dead? Any person who has already passed away and who you consider you have a bond with. The bond can be a family bond: any relative who has died, whether you met them or not. The bond can be the family you chose: friends and partners who have passed away. The bond can be spiritual: mentors and important figures of your spiritual tradition who have died. The bond can be to your community: guardians of the

CONSEJO

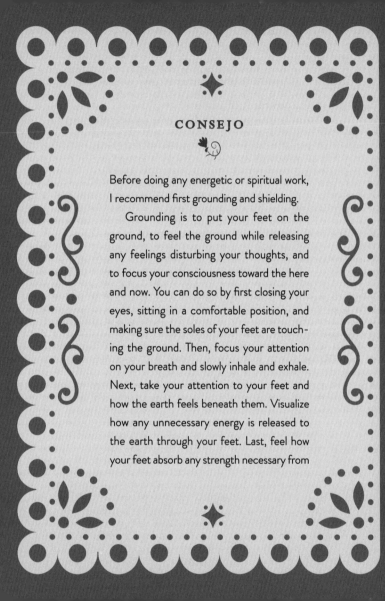

Before doing any energetic or spiritual work, I recommend first grounding and shielding.

Grounding is to put your feet on the ground, to feel the ground while releasing any feelings disturbing your thoughts, and to focus your consciousness toward the here and now. You can do so by first closing your eyes, sitting in a comfortable position, and making sure the soles of your feet are touching the ground. Then, focus your attention on your breath and slowly inhale and exhale. Next, take your attention to your feet and how the earth feels beneath them. Visualize how any unnecessary energy is released to the earth through your feet. Last, feel how your feet absorb any strength necessary from the earth. Take a few breaths, and whenever you are ready, open your eyes to the here and now.

Shielding is to visualize an energetic magical shield of protection around you. You can do so by first closing your eyes, sitting in a comfortable position, and focusing your attention on your breath. Then, take your attention to your heart, the source of life and love. Feel the love you have for yourself, for life itself, for others, and for your spiritual guides, spirits, or deities. Visualize this love as a strong white light pouring from your heart. Picture how this light starts growing, covering your entire body. It reaches the distance of your arms outstretched, until you are covered by white light and within a white egg of light. You are within love, you are safe, and no harm can enter this space.

land, leaders, and public figures who contributed something that you are grateful for.

Can you only include humans in the Day of the Dead altar? The answer is no. Although the Day of the Dead is focused mainly on humans, some people include their pets as well, adding pictures of their dogs, cats, or any animal companions they deeply miss.

If you are fortunate and do not have any person who has died and had a bond with, you can create your Day of the Day altar with the other elements and dedicate it to the spirits who need it: those who have died and do not have someone to pray for them or remember them, those who died in a recent natural disaster, those who used to live on the land you live in, and others you would like to honor and express your gratitude to.

Whom to include and whom not to? If you are wondering if you should include someone you did not get along with—for example, an uncle who was mean to you—I would advise thinking twice. It would not be right or wrong, but make sure you are including each person out of respect and love. In the end, it depends on you, as you are the host of the party. Nothing bad would happen, but you would probably not feel comfortable or would not create the altar from a loving space. Nonetheless, grounding and shielding would help you when doing so (see page 70).

(see page 70)

· ACTIVIDAD 3 ·
Creating a Family Tree

The best way to start learning about your family's history and your ancestors is by creating a family tree. Grab a big piece of paper and a pen and start by writing down your name at the bottom of the piece of paper and the names of any siblings next to you. Then, write the name of your parents above your siblings and you. Next, write down the names of your parents' siblings next to them and the names of your grandparents above them, and then your grandparents' siblings and parents. Fill in any of your siblings' descendants below their names. Draw a non-touching horizontal line between siblings, touching horizontal lines between couples, and a vertical line between parents and their offspring. Mark the people that have passed away with a sign: for example, RIP.

The people above you with RIP are your ancestors. All the people marked with the RIP letters are the people that you can celebrate on the Day of the Dead, along with dead friends and other dead unrelated people you knew and cared about. The rest of the people, who are alive, are not included in the *ofrenda*.

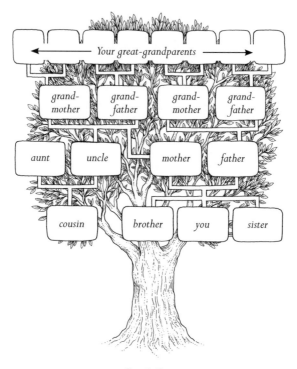

Family Tree

• ACTIVIDAD 4 •
Choosing the Right Place

Now that you have your guest list ready, the next phase of the festivity preparation is choosing the venue. However, because in this case the location is your own home, selecting the location consists of choosing the part of your home and the surface or furniture you are going to use as the base. If possible, it should be a space that is going to be mainly dedicated to the Day of the Dead festivity.

Think of where you usually host your parties and welcome your ordinary guests. The place where the best moments are spent is probably the living room or the dining room. I like placing my altar in the dining room so we can sit next to the altar and for the living to enjoy our own feast while next to us the dead enjoy theirs. However, if for some reason this is not possible, you can use any other indoor place in your home, such as your bedroom. I strongly suggest not to use your bathroom or a cleaning storage room, as it would not be a respectful place to receive special guests. Keep away from anything that may catch fire.

Regarding the surface or piece of furniture, you can use any table or desk you can afford not to use for a

CONSEJO

Just like when you are about to receive living guests into your home, it is a good occasion to clean and dust off your house to make it as presentable and comfortable as possible. Throw out anything that you do not need anymore.

I usually deep clean my house before an important holiday because I like to create a comfortable space for the intention of the holiday.

period of time. I personally prefer using my console dining room table, but you can use any elevated structure, like a fireplace mantel, a coffee table, or even a bedside table in your room.

Once you have selected the place of your home and the furniture you will use, carefully move the furniture if needed, placing it against a wall to minimize the risk of someone bumping into it and knocking over items. I also recommend avoiding placing it near a window or where there is usually a lot of airflow; this is to avoid items of the altar falling down constantly because of the air.

Gathering Your Altar Items

Once you have your list of guests ready, you know where you will place your altar, and your home is ready for the celebration, it is time to start collecting everything you will need for the *ofrenda*.

I recommend starting to collect the items a few weeks before the celebration, around mid-October. Some items are easy to get; you can use water right from the tap. Others will require more time and effort to get them, like collecting and curating the pictures of the deceased. Some will require a bit of spending, like flowers and candles. A few will require more time and planning: for example, if you plan to cook something special or make *pan de muerto*.

Agua (Water)

Water represents the source of life and the purity of the soul. It is offered to the souls for them to quench their thirst after their long journey. The water is also reminiscent of the Tlalocan, the first level of the Aztec underworld, a happy place, humid and full of vegetation, ruled by the Aztec god of rain and water, Tláloc.

You can use tap water from your home. You will need a container for the water. The traditional material of the cups or glasses is clay, but you can also use glass.

You can include the element water in your altar with a single cup of water or with several cups of water. I usually place three to four cups of water around the altar. During the days of the festivity, it is important to keep an eye on the water and refill or refresh if necessary. Do not drink from this water—it is for the deceased only.

Bebidas y Tabaco (Drinks and Tobacco)

One custom is to add liquors and tobacco to the Day of the Dead altars to represent the vices of the dead loved ones.

CONSEJO

I recommend making a list around early October based on the list on page 66. First, check what you have already available at home. Then, categorize the items that you would need to get. Last, create a few subcategories for the items that you can get without needing to spend money, like the pictures if you are planning to ask your relatives for them, and the items that you would need to buy, like candles.

You can add to the altar your loved ones' favorite drinks. For example, if your grandfather loved wine, you can include a glass of his favorite wine. If he used to smoke cigars, you can include one cigar next to his picture.

Traditionally, the offered drinks are made from the *muguey* (agave) plant: pulque, tequila, or mezcal. Pulque is the ancestor of drinks, made from fermenting the sap of the *maguey*. An old legend mentions that pulque was used by the god Tezcatlipoca to trick and get the god Quetzalcóatl drunk.

Making tequila and mezcal includes a distillation process. Mezcal is mainly produced in the state of Oaxaca. It is considered to be the drink of heavens, and the legend says it was first made by a bolt of lightning that hit the *maguey*. It is widely used in parties, ceremonies, and *limpias* (traditional cleansing ceremonies). It is offered to the four cardinal points and the earth before

Traditionally, the offered drinks are made from zthe *muguey* (agave) plant: pulque, tequila, or mezcal.

drinking. In some parts of the state, it is sprayed on tombs during the Day of the Dead to give a farewell to the souls.

Calaveritas de Azúcar (Sugar Skulls)

The *calaveras* (or *calaveritas*, "little skulls") are decorative and edible skulls. They are usually made of sugar, although they are also made of chocolate and amaranth. They represent the deceased and the ever-present death. Generally, small sugar skulls are placed to represent the deceased and a bigger skull or skulls to represent death and the Divine. Sugar skulls are also given as gifts to family and friends, and they serve as a sign of affection and a reminder of our mortality. The *calavera* usually has a name on its forehead to represent the person it is given to or a deceased person when placed at an altar.

The origin of the *calaveras* is the *tzompantli*, which means "rows of heads." The *tzompantli* were walls of several rows of skulls of the sacrificed that were located in important temples to honor the gods.

If you are not able to buy sugar skulls, you can use any figure with the shape of a human skull, or you can make your own.

Making Calaveritas de Azúcar (Sugar Skulls)

This recipe makes 6 sugar skulls.

For the Skulls

1 egg white

Vanilla

2 teaspoons corn syrup

Lime juice

4 cups confectioner's sugar

For the Icing

2 cups confectioner's sugar

2 tablespoons meringue powder

3 tablespoons warm water

½ teaspoon vanilla

Gel food coloring of choice

Edible glitter (optional)

Creating the Skulls

1. In a bowl whisk the egg white, vanilla, corn syrup, and a few drops of lime juice. Then slowly add the confectioners' sugar through a sieve.

2. Mix all the ingredients with a spatula or your hands until a dry dough is formed, and then divide it into 6 equal parts.

3. Start shaping your dough in the form of a skull. You can use your fingers to create the eye cavities and the tip of a paintbrush to make the nose. If the dough feels too dry to shape, you can add a few extra drops of lime juice.

4. Once you have all your skulls ready, let them dry for at least 3 hours.

5. Using a stand mixer at medium-low speed, begin making the icing by mixing the sugar and meringue powder. Then slowly add the water and vanilla. Increase the speed to medium and mix until stiff peaks form, about 5 to 10 minutes.

6. Divide the icing into equal parts, depending on how many colors you want to make, and then add food coloring to each. Start with just a few drops and mix well. If need be, add more until you reach the hue you desire. Go all-out and use lots of bright colors.

7. Scoop each color into different piping bags fitted with a size 2 or 3 tip and start decorating your skulls. You can also use a small plastic baggy with a corner cut off. If you want to add more flair to your *calaveritas de azúcar,* you can add edible glitter to decorate the eye sockets.

Calaveritas

Comida (Food)

Besides the other edible items mentioned in this chapter, the *calaveritas* and the *pan de muerto,* another custom is adding your dead loved ones' favorite dishes. The food is offered to delight the souls. Traditional food added to the altars includes *mole* and chocolate.

You can cook your loved ones' favorite dishes or the traditional food of your region and add small portions on your altar. Smaller portions of food that is usually enjoyed by kids, like candy or small sweet bread, are usually offered to the children's souls. You can include special beverages for them, like juice, next to their pictures.

If you have pets and are worried about leaving food unattended, you can use real food for the setting of the altar and calling the loved ones and later replace it with fake food made of modeling clay or plastic. You would not like your cat climbing on your altar, attracted by the smell, and eating something that could be dangerous for it.

• ACTIVIDAD 6 •
Making Calabaza en Tacha
(Candied Pumpkin)

The pumpkin is the classic icon of autumn. Pumpkins are greatly cultivated in southern and eastern Mexico and have been eaten and cooked since pre-Hispanic times. As the pumpkin is harvested around October, it is widely incorporated into the traditional and seasonal dishes. One of the emblematic desserts of the celebration is the *calabaza en tacha*, candied pumpkin. The following recipe yields 7 servings.

Ingredients

4¼ cups water

2.2 pounds *piloncillo* or dark brown sugar

4 cloves

2 cinnamon sticks

2 star anise

2 oranges, sliced

4.4-pound butternut squash or sugar pumpkin, cleaned and sliced into wedges

4 guavas, quartered

Sesame seeds (optional)

1. In a pot on medium-low heat, dissolve the water and *piloncillo* with the cloves, cinnamon, and star anise.

2. Add the orange and cook for about 5 minutes. Then throw in the pumpkin slices and the guava and let them cook for another 35 to 40 minutes or until the pumpkin is cooked through. Times can vary depending on the variety of pumpkin you choose.

3. Let it cool and serve. You can add sesame seeds to decorate.

Copal and Incense

Copal is an aromatic tree resin from a tree with the same name, copal tree, of the Burseraceae family, and is endemic to warm and humid regions of Mexico and Central America. Copal was used as an offering by the indigenous pre-Hispanic people to their gods and was also used for medical purposes or to purify participants before rituals. When burned, the copal produces white smoke swirls called *iztac teteo* ("white gods"). The smoke was seen as a channel of communication between humans and gods. The copal used to be buried as an offering, for it to be constantly used by the gods. Incense was introduced later by the Spanish conquerors.

The copal on the Day of the Dead altar represents an offering to the gods or spirits, and the sweet aroma attracts and calls the dead. It elevates the prayer or ritual, and it is also used to cleanse the space so the souls can enter safely.

You will need an incense holder or an ash catcher for your incense. Copal is traditionally burnt on a *sahumerio* or *copalera*, which has the shape of a cup and is made out of clay.

CONSEJO

If there is no copal in your area, you can search for a sweet and light resin or an herb that is soothing and usually used for meditation or cleansing purposes, such as sandalwood, frankincense, sage, or palo santo. You can also use incense wood sticks of one of these aromas.

Flores (Flowers): Cempasúchil (Mexican Marigold)

Flowers are an important element of the Day of the Dead altar. They are not only used as decoration, but they are also an offering. They represent life and death, their aroma attracts the dead, and their petals are used to trace a path to guide the spirits.

The *cempasúchil*, the Mexican marigold, is a plant from the *Tagetes* genus. The name *cempasúchil* comes from the Nahuatl *cempohualxochitl*, which means "twenty flowers," "flower of twenty petals," or "many flowers." There are more than thirty species of this flower in Mexico. It is used to dye textiles, as an insecticide, and for its multiple medicinal properties. However, it is commonly known as the "flower of the dead," as it is one of the main symbols of the festivity.

The *cempasúchil* flower is harvested in early October, when the rainy season is coming to an end, just in time for the Day of the Dead. Because of their strong yellow and orange colors, they also represent the sun. They are placed on Day of the Dead altars and on tombs to provide warmth, and their petals are usually used to trace a path between the cemeteries and the homes to guide the dead to the altars. Their strong aroma guides the dead to their destiny.

In my family, we notice the scent of these flowers when someone close is about to die. Accompanied by a nostalgic feeling, out of nowhere we smell the very particular scent of these flowers. We look around and there are no flowers nearby. We call each other: one person says, "I'm smelling—" and the other interrupts, saying, "The flowers. Yes. Me too . . . someone is about to leave." We have this "sensation" for days until we receive the news, the call announcing that someone close has died.

Other flowers used for the Day of the Dead are the *nube*, baby's breath (*Gypsophila muralis*), because of their white color that represents purity, and the *terciopelo,* the cockscomb flower (*Celosia argentea*), which blooms in September and comes in a variety of red, white, and yellow colors.

It would be lovely if you could collect the flowers yourself in your garden or in nearby fields, but this is not possible in many urban areas. I usually go to a famous market in Mexico City, the Jamaica Market, which is known for its wide flower selection with accessible prices.

If there are no marigolds available where you live, you can use any other type of flower, like chrysanthemum or forget-me-not, both used as symbols of death and

CONSEJO

Try collecting or buying flowers on the day of or day before setting up your altar. You would not like to put withered flowers on your altar, as the flowers need to be fresh, colorful, and have a pleasant aroma at the time of welcoming your guests.

It's important to get fresh flowers because the smell guides your ancestors to the sacred place of your altar. If you are going to set your altar on October 31 or November 1, then I suggest you plan to collect the fresh flowers around October 29 or 30.

mourning in many regions of the world. You can also use roses, for example, which are usually abundant during the summer, or carnations, which are usually available all year round in temperate regions.

I recommend using flowers that are abundantly available at the time of the celebration, as it is a festivity linked to the change of the season and to the harvest. I suggest investigating what flowers are typical in your area around this time of the year (autumn: late October to early November) and using flowers with strong yellow or orange colors and a strong aroma.

• ACTIVIDAD 7 •
Making Paper Marigold Flowers

If you are not able to collect or buy flowers, you can also make your own. Try making marigold flowers using paper. You can include them along with natural flowers to decorate your altar and home or to replace natural flowers if you are not able to get them. You can also save them for your future Day of the Dead celebrations.

See illustrations on pages 94 and 95 for folding help.

Materials

Orange or yellow crepe or tissue paper (1 sheet
    per flower)

Scissors

Ruler

Pencil or pen

Green pipe cleaner or wire (1 per flower)

Start by cutting small squares or rectangles of paper 3
to 4 inches long with the scissors. You can use the ruler
and pen to measure the size, if needed. Then, put one
rectangle on top of the other to make piles of 6 to 8 rectangles each. Fold one side inward about ½ inch, flip over
and fold the same side inward, and repeat until you've
made an accordion.

Now, grab the pipe cleaner or wire and wrap one end
tightly around the middle of the accordion. Cut the edges
of the accordion in the form of small semicircles or triangles. Pinking shears or other craft scissors are helpful for
this step. Open the accordion so the sides touch, and sep-
arate each layer of paper until they form a dome shape.
The flower is ready!

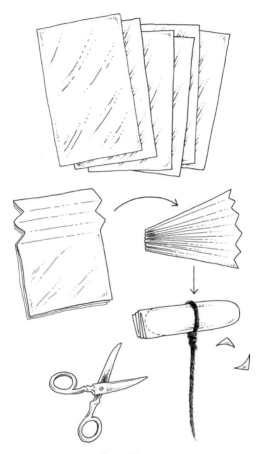

Paper Flowers

Paper Flowers (continued)

chapter three

Fotos de los Difuntos
(Pictures of the Deceased)

A very important item on your Day of the Dead altar is the pictures of the deceased. These represent the dead loved ones to whom you are dedicating your *ofrenda*.

Gather pictures for each dead guest that you have included in your guest list. You can ask for help from your family members, and it would be a good opportunity to visit them, if possible, and go through family albums together.

In my family and other families I know, the owners of family albums and pictures are usually very protective of them, so I recommend inviting them to come with you to make a copy of the pictures, or assuring them you only need them to make a copy and will return the pictures as soon as possible. You can also take a picture right there with your mobile phone, if possible, and then print it. If you tell them why you need the photos and that you are preparing a Day of the Dead altar to honor them, your relatives will hopefully be touched and understand the situation better.

Gather pictures for each dead guest included in your guest list.

You can also search through social media and print the pictures if you cannot find anything already printed. If you cannot find any picture of your loved one, you can also use paintings, make a drawing, or write the full name of the person on a card with the dates of birth and death.

Try to select pictures with a portrait style, in which only the deceased appears in the picture. I try to avoid using pictures with people who are still alive. It is said that a picture carries the energy of the person, so I try to only include the people I am honoring. You can include pictures of couples or groups of people if all the people who appear in the picture have died.

The pictures can show the people younger than when you last saw them, or they can appear just as you remember them. They can be doing something they enjoyed while they were alive, like riding a horse or dancing, or they can just be posing in front of the camera. The most important thing is that the picture reflects your memory of their personality, of their essence.

However, sometimes it is hard to find the perfect picture, especially for loved ones who passed a long time ago. I only have one picture of my great-grandparents. I do not have options to choose from, but I feel very happy

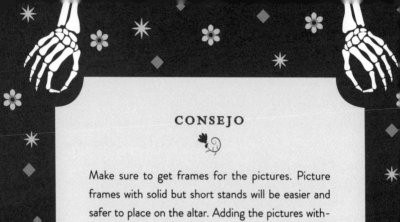

CONSEJO

Make sure to get frames for the pictures. Picture frames with solid but short stands will be easier and safer to place on the altar. Adding the pictures without a frame can damage them, or they can keep falling down.

If you do not have enough frames for your pictures or if this falls out of your budget, I recommend using upside-down binder clips to hold the pictures.

and fortunate to have any picture of them and be able to use it for my *ofrenda*.

You can also include multiple pictures in which the same deceased person appears. For example, I usually include a picture of my grandmother with her siblings, as I do not have other pictures of her siblings. I also include one of her alone, smiling at the camera; it reminds me of how her smile made me feel happy and safe. I include another one in which she and my grandfather are hugging each other, and the picture reminds me of their love, which originated my father's life and mine. And I also include one of my grandfather alone, raising his glass of wine toward the camera like making a toast. The picture reminds me of all the family gatherings and how he always used to make a toast and say a few words of love and hope, and when looking at the altar and the picture, I feel like I'm toasting with him.

• ACTIVIDAD 8 •
Collecting Pictures of Our Ancestors

A family activity that I have always enjoyed is looking at family photo albums with my parents and my brother and sisters. We sit down at the table and pass on each picture, one by one. Our father or our mother tells us the story of each picture, and if we do not know who is on the picture, we ask and they explain. We remember our childhood and we talk about those who have left us. Through the stories we tell, we remember those who have left us and we honor their lives. By talking about our family's past, we also understand better our present.

Ask your relatives for pictures of your ancestors and gather pictures of all the loved ones that you want to include in your Day of the Dead altar. Make collecting pictures a family activity. Tell the stories you know or ask relatives to share some favorites. Make a copy of the pictures you like so you'll have them for future occasions.

Juguetes y Objetos Personales de los Difuntos (Toys and Personal Items of the Deceased)

In pre-Hispanic times, people's remains were usually buried with some of their personal objects. The dead were endowed for their travel according to their social categories, given items such as weapons, jewelry, figures, masks, and vases made of clay.

You can include in the altar small objects that were owned by the deceased or objects that are related to the life they lived. These can be some of their favorite objects that can fit into the altar: for example, you can include your grandfather's favorite watch next to his picture or your aunt's necklace in front of hers. They can be objects related to their passions or professions: for example, a stethoscope for your uncle who was a doctor, a pen for a friend who loved to write, or a clown's red nose for your partner who loved entertaining and making kids laugh.

If any little dead loved ones are included in the altar, you can add some of their favorite toys.

Pan de Muerto (Bread of the Dead)

Many of the offerings found on the Day of the Dead altar represent the body of the dead. For example, for the indigenous Nahua people from Cuetzalan, Puebla, the *tamales* represent the body of the dead: the leaves wrapping the dough represent the coffin, the dough represents the flesh, and the *mole* sauce representing the body fluids.

The *pan de muerto*, the bread of the dead, represents the dead, the cycle of life and death, and the cardinal points. Like the sugar skull, it is both decorative and edible.

The most common food found on the Day of the Dead altar is *pan de muerto*. There are several types of *pan de muerto*, and they can vary from region to region.

However, most of them have the shape of the human body. The common *pan de muerto* found in urban centers has a bun shape with a ball in the center ringed by four bone-shaped long lines, symbolizing a skull surrounded by skeletal remains pointing to each cardinal point, as a representation of where the gods Quetzalcóatl, Tlaloc, Xipe Totec, and Tezcatlipoca are located.

Pre-Hispanic people used to make a type of tortilla with the shape of butterflies or lightning for offerings. For example, these types of offerings were left in temples or crossroads as a dedication to the *cihuapipiltin*, the noblewomen, divine spirits of women who died during childbirth.

However, the exact origin of the *pan de muerto* is unclear. One version says that the *pan de muerto* was born as a substitution used by the Spanish conquerors for a ritual where, after sacrificing an Aztec princess, the beating heart was put in a pot full of amaranth and was later eaten as a sign of gratitude. As the Spanish people did not like these types of rituals, their solution was to create a bread made of wheat flour sprinkled with red-colored sugar to simulate blood. Another version states that it comes from the Catholic tradition of All Saints' Day, when saints' relics, including bones, were worshipped and candy and bread were made with the shape of these relics.

• ACTIVIDAD 9 •
Baking Pan de Muerto

Ingredients

¼ cup milk

15 grams instant yeast (about 2¼ ¼-ounce packets)

4 cups flour

6⅓ tablespoons (80 grams) sugar, plus extra for glaze

4 eggs

2 teaspoons orange blossom water

2.82 ounces (80 grams) butter, plus extra for glaze

pinch of salt

1. In a bowl combine the milk and instant yeast and let it rest.

2. In a large bowl pour the flour and make a well in the middle. Inside the well add the sugar, eggs, orange blossom water, and the yeast-milk mixture. And on the outside of the well, sprinkle the pinch of salt to avoid it being in direct contact with the yeast.

3. Start mixing all the ingredients from the inside out until a dough forms.

4. Add the butter at room temperature and continue kneading until all the ingredients are completely incorporated and the dough is smooth and fluffy. Add the necessary flour so the dough doesn't stick to your hands.

5. Cover the dough with a clean, damp dishcloth and let it rise in a warm area until it doubles its size.

6. Once the resting period is over, reserve approximately ¼ of the dough to make the bone shapes.

7. Portion the remaining dough into 3 or 4 equal-size flat-bottomed semi-spheres.

8. To shape the round bone at the top of your loaf, make smaller spheres. For the longer ones on the sides, roll the dough into small logs and gently apply pressure with your fingers to form the shape of the bones.

9. Position the bone shapes on the loaves and press gently so they adhere. Let them rest in a warm place so they can double in size for about an hour.

10. Preheat your oven to 350°F and bake for about 40 minutes or until golden brown.

11. Let them cool briefly, glaze them with melted butter, and sprinkle them with white sugar.

Pan de Muerto

Papel Picado (Cut Colored Paper)

Papel picado is a colorful, light paper cut or perforated with different shapes. It represents the element air and the joy of the festivity. When the paper is moved by air, it is said that it is announcing the spirits' arrival.

Papel picado is also used in other celebrations and to decorate homes and streets. It has a pre-Hispanic origin, as the Aztec people used paper made of tree bark to decorate their temples. Tissue paper was introduced from China to Mexico in the eighteenth century. In the nineteenth century, workers from the state of Puebla used it to wrap products that were sold in the stores of the *haciendas,* and they started making pieces of art with it. It was later spread to other states in the twentieth century.

• ACTIVIDAD 10 •
Making Your Own Papel Picado

You will need tissue paper or any other type of thin and light paper in different colors, scissors, yarn, and masking tape. Common paper colors used are orange, pink, yellow, green, and blue. If you cannot find tissue paper, you can choose any type of thin paper that is colorful and light. If you are not able to use paper, you can also use colorful and light fabric such as tablecloths.

Start by cutting the paper to make rectangles that are 8 inches wide and 12 inches long, or about the size of a standard piece of paper if that's more convenient.

Now, fold the piece of paper in half like a book, and fold it again in half until you have a long vertical rectangle. Then, round the bottom side of the rectangle, cutting off the corners, to make a half-circle facing downward. Next, cut little shapes on the left and right edges of the rectangle. You can cut triangles, squares, or half-circles. Use additional folds to create a pattern to your liking. Unfold your piece of paper and you will have symmetric shapes: your *papel picado* is ready!

You can use the pieces of *papel picado* to cover the surface of the altar and to create hanging garlands to decorate your altar and home. Hang the pieces of paper from the facing edge of the table, securing them from the top with masking tape or with doubled-faced tape. You can also hang them as banners from wall to wall with a cord or yarn, using tape to attach the papers to the string and the string to the walls.

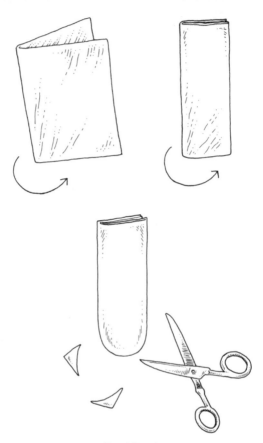

Papel Picado

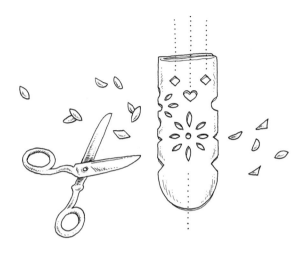

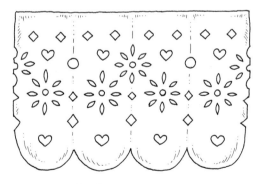

Papel Picado (continued)

Sal (Salt)

The salt in an altar usually represents the element earth. On the Day of the Dead *ofrenda* it represents purification.

It is usually placed in a little bowl. Salt or flower petals are also spread on the center of the altar in the shape of a cross, pointing to each cardinal direction to help with the spirits' orientation.

You can use any type of salt, but try using white salt to represent purification. I prefer using sea salt in comparison to regular table salt, as it is more natural: it comes directly from the evaporation of seawater and has not been processed or has gone through minimal processing. Also, the sea salt crystal size is bigger and is easier to manage.

Velas (Candles)

Candles represent fire, light, hope, and faith. The light guides the spirits on their way back home. Pre-Hispanic people used sticks of *ocote* wood, especially flammable wood from the Montezuma pine.

The candles used for the Day of the Dead altar are usually white, although other colors can sometimes be found—for example, purple would represent grief.

Traditionally, one candle is placed for each dead loved one. However, if you are remembering several loved ones, I recommended not to put too many candles on your home altar for safety purposes. You can also put one to three bigger candles to act as main lights, dedicated to your deity or spirit or to guide all the spirits.

I use votive candles for the deceased, and I include bigger candles such as pillar candles for Spirit or deities. If your altar or table is small, you can use tea light candles and votive candles.

I suggest selecting candles in glass containers. Clear glass also allows the white color to remain visible. Containing the burning candle protects the altar surface, flowers, paper, and tablecloths from the flame. Remember to never leave a flame unattended.

You may want to stock extra candles, especially if you select little ones. This way you can light the first batch when setting up the altar and welcoming your loved ones and then light the extras when doing the meditation at your altar and when saying goodbye.

Other Symbols of the Day of the Dead
Árbol de la Muerte (Tree of Death)

Trees of death are chandeliers made of clay, originally made in Metepec, Estado de Mexico. They represent the life that continues after death. They include symbols like

CONSEJO

Although some people prefer to leave the candles lit until they burn out. I strongly recommend to not leave any candles unattended. Put out lit candles before going to sleep or before leaving your house. Light them again the next morning, when you come back home, or when you are going to be near the altar. Safety first!

If you cannot light candles at home because of safety reasons, use flameless candles.

flowers, leaves, and birds, which represent life and fertility and their counterparts death and scarcity.

El Papalote (The Kite)

A kite consists of a light frame covered with a thin material, a piece of paper or fabric, that is attached to a long thread and is flown and moved by the wind. In Mexico and some regions of Latin America, we use the word *papalote* to refer to a kite. The word comes from the Nahuatl *papalotl,* which means "butterfly."

A tradition from the state of Oaxaca is to fly kites to guide the dead during their journey. A few days before the Day of the Dead, kites are flown to show the dead the way to their homes, believing the souls go down through the threads. After the festivities, the kites are flown again to show them their way back.

• ACTIVIDAD 11 •
Creating and Flying a Kite

Materials

Small handsaw or utility knife

2 sticks, such as wooden dowels, one slightly larger than
    the other (for example, 20 and 12 inches)

Long thread, around 60 feet long (reel of cotton thread
    recommended)

Scissors

Masking tape

1 large sheet of paper (for example, 30 by 20 inches),
such as newspaper or tissue paper

Ribbon, 60 inches long

1. Use a small handsaw or utility knife to carve notches
   in the end of the sticks so that the string stays put in
   step 5. If making this craft with kids, do this step
   for them.

2. Set the longer stick down on your work surface,
   pointing it away from you.

3. Center the shorter one so that it is perpendicular
   to the longer one, $^2/_3$ of the way along the longer
   stick, creating a lowercase t shape.

4. With the string, tie the sticks together where they
   meet.

5. Pull the string upward and through the top notch.
   Then pull the string to each of the ends, laying it in
   each notch, and tie the string, keeping it stretched
   and creating a diamond shape. Tie off the string.
   Your frame is done!

6. With a small and light piece of masking tape, rein-
   force the intersection of the sticks.

7. Put the frame on top of the piece of paper and cut around the paper about 1 to 2 inches from the edge of the frame.

8. Fold the edges of the paper over the string and secure the edges with the masking tape.

9. Tie a long string to the reinforced intersection.

10. Tie or paste the ribbon to the bottom point to create the tail.

Now that your kite is ready, wait for the ideal time to go out. Go to a big open space. It can be a park, a beach, or a big garden, with not many trees or power lines. Make sure it's safe—avoid places where cars pass by, and do not fly your kite if there is rain and lightning.

It will be better if a friend or relative helps you launch your kite. This person will hold the kite facing you, walking about 50 feet away, while you hold the string line taut. If you are alone or if you have a helper, you'll need to have your back facing the wind, and when you feel the kite is catching the wind, slowly release the kite and slowly let out the line. Avoid running when launching your kite, and when the kite is gaining height, draw the kite's line to you.

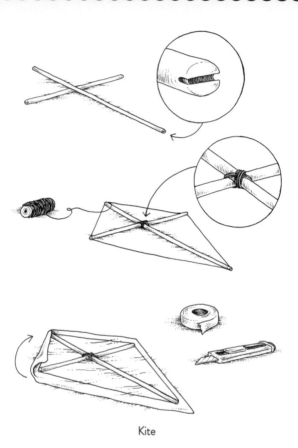

Kite

Kite (continued)

CONSEJO

Adding a tail to the kite provides stability. The tail's length should be at least three times the length of the kite.

Decorate your kite's paper and tail with figures that are special for you or with the names of your dead loved ones and ancestors.

La Catrina

Death is commonly represented by a smiling skull or skeleton. *La Catrina* is one of the most famous icons and representations of death. It was created at the beginning of the Mexican Revolution by the artist José Guadalupe Posada as a satirical portrait of the rich of the late nineteenth and early twentieth centuries, who liked pretending to have another lifestyle. The Catrina, originally called *la Calavera Garbancera*, is all skin and bones but is wearing a modern European hat. Later, in the 1940s, the painter Diego Rivera included the character in his painting *Dream of a Sunday Afternoon in the Alameda Central,* with other figures of the time. Rivera also coined the name *Catrina*.

• ACTIVIDAD 12 •
Catrina Face Painting

This activity is intended to be a tribute to the symbol of the Catrina, as representation or characterization of death, rather than used as a scary costume. You will need white, black, and bright-colored makeup and black eyeliner.

Start by outlining a circled line around each eye, surrounding both the eye and the eyebrow with one big circle. Outline a triangle on the point of the nose.

Then, cover the entire face with the white makeup, avoiding the areas defined by the eyeliner. Next, with black makeup, cover the eyes and the tip of the nose, and paint some lines above and below the lips representing the skull's teeth. Finally, with the black and bright colored makeup, add lines or curves in the forehead and cheeks. You can add colorful flowers around the eyes and even wear a crown of flowers.

El Xolo (The Xoloitzcuintli Dog)

The Xoloitzcuintli, or Xolo, is also known as the Mexican hairless dog. The name comes from *Xólotl* (Aztec god of death) and *itzcuintli* (Nahuatl for "dog"). It is one of the most ancient dog breeds, and its history goes back 3,500 years. After the Spanish Conquest, Xolo dogs almost became extinct, until the mid-twentieth century, when they were found in non-urban areas in the states of Oaxaca and Guerrero. Artists like Diego Rivera and Frida Kahlo boosted their popularity, as they owned some Xolos and included them in some of their paintings. It is said that the dog god Xólotl created the Xolo to guide the souls' journey through the Mictlán. The Nahua and Maya used to include dogs in their burials, to guide the spirit of the deceased (de la Garza 2014). Similarly, some people include a clay or ceramic figure of a Xolo on their altars, for it to keep company and guide their loved ones, or to represent their dead dogs.

La Mariposa Monarca (The Monarch Butterfly)

The monarch butterfly is seen as a symbol of the festivity of the dead. Every year in October and November, the monarch butterfly starts to arrive in Mexico in the states of Michoacán and Estado de Mexico after a very long journey from the northern regions of the continent. They are respected and seen as sacred, as the souls of the dead announcing their visit, the spirits of nature, and messengers of the gods.

The Ofrenda in a Nutshell

The Day of the Day altar, or *ofrenda,* is a temporary sacred space dedicated to honoring and celebrating your dead loved ones and ancestors during the celebration. The *ofrendas* are usually set in homes, but there are altars created by the community. They are representations of the universe, the connection between earth and heaven. They are also a place for offerings. The *ofrenda* includes several symbols or items, and the preparation of the altar consists of gathering and placing them.

Making a list of your dead loved ones and ancestors helps you define who you are going to dedicate the celebration to. Cleaning your home before the arrival of your guests makes sure your house is ready for them, and preparing the space helps to make sure you have the right atmosphere for the celebration.

Gather the items you will need for your altar: water, to represent life and purity; drinks and tobacco, to symbolize the vices of your dead loved ones; skulls, to represent death and the dead; food, to give as an offering; incense, to give as an offering and to purify the space; flowers, to give as an offering and to guide the spirits; pictures of your ancestors and dead loved ones, to remember them and represent their presence; toys, for the souls of the children; personal items of the deceased, to entertain them; bread, to represent the body of the dead and give as an offering; colorful light paper, to represent the wind that announces the dead's arrival; salt, to represent purification and to orient to each cardinal point with a cross; and candles, to guide the spirits back home.

Other symbols may ••• represent death to ••• you, such as the butterfly.

If you cannot find the specific items mentioned in this chapter, you can look for others that represent the same meaning and that are available in your region and abundant during this time of the year, autumn. Other symbols may represent death or the dead to you, such as the butterfly. If there are other items you may want to include as an offering to your dead loved ones, feel free to add these to your altar.

Chapter Four

CELEBRATING
THE DAY
OF THE DEAD

You have learned how to prepare for the Day of the Dead and you have gathered the items that you will need. You now need to set the space for the celebration. Setting the *ofrenda* is a ritual on its own. When putting each item on the altar, we are summoning what each represents, and when placing the pictures of each of our dead loved ones, we are inviting them to join us.

I recommend first setting up the altar carefully with each of the items, and then doing the ritual I describe in *actividad* 16 (see page 141).

In Cuentepec, Temixco, located in the state of Morelos (South Central Mexico), each phase of the Day of the Dead festivity has a name and specific activity. Two weeks before the Day of the Dead, on October 18 (St. Luke's Day), they welcome their dead loved ones and put out a glass of water and simple food for them to recover after their journey. This day is called *Kin kakawa mimike,* which means "they let the dead go out." They believe their dead loved ones arrive exhausted after their travel from Mictlán.

The *Mekailwitl*, which means "the days before the Feast of the Dead," is the time people gather and buy the elements needed for the altar and festivity. The setting of the altar is called *techia,* which means "the wait." It is not only the physical act of placing the items on the altar, but also the act of calling upon the loved ones, naming them, remembering them, and talking to them.

The *Tetsatsilia*, which means "the call," is the formal invitation to the dead loved ones. It is usually done by one person, usually a woman. The rest of the people quietly sit down around the altar showing respect. The *Tetsatsilia* consists of naming each of the dead guests one by one, placing a candle for each, and offering the altar's food and beverages to them (Domingo Olivares 2016, 40–43).

• ACTIVIDAD 13 •
Setting Up the Day of the Dead Altar

Traditionally, the Day of the Dead altar is set up on the night of October 31 or right before November 1, just before the holiday. However, some people, like myself, set it up a few weeks before the Day of the Dead; this way I can enjoy the altar, after the effort of setting it up, a bit longer.

Start by removing any objects from the surface that you are going to use as the base of your altar and relocating them to another place where you can leave them for some days. Dust off the surface and clean it with a damp cloth, taking precautions depending on the material of the surface.

Cleanse your home and altar by burning some copal or incense or by smudging with a cleansing herb such as sage. Move around your home, starting at the top and finishing at the bottom. Walk across each room in a clockwise direction until you get to the main entrance of your home. From the main entrance move directly to the altar and cleanse the altar's space and surface.

Cover the surface with a plastic bag or with a plastic tablecloth to protect the surface. If your altar includes water and it is spilled, the water can damage the surface of the table or the colored paper, or the flower petals can stain. You can cover the plastic with a thin fabric table-cloth in a traditional color, white or black. It is important to avoid having wrinkles in the tablecloths, as they can affect the stability of any items placed on top of them. Over the tablecloth, place the sheets of *papel picado*. You can place them in lines, centered and equidistant from each other.

Then, put the picture frames on the altar. Place them on the back of the altar and leave an empty space in the center of the altar and on the front. You can make groups of picture frames, gathering the people who knew each other when they were alive. For example, you can place your maternal relatives on one side and your paternal ones on the other, or your family on one side and your friends on the other. Add any religious or spiritual figures or symbols you want to include with the picture frames or groups of frames.

CONSEJO

If you want to set up an *ofrenda* with different levels, you can use thick paperboards or strong boxes for the different levels and place each on top of the other, the biggest one on the bottom and the smallest one on top. You can use a table or the biggest box as the base. Then cover the boxes with colored paper or with light tablecloths.

Traditionally, the first level (the highest level) is used for the religious or spiritual figures. The last level (the closest to the ground) is used to guide the dead: it holds the flower petals or a cross with salt or flowers. For the other levels in between, you can either mix the other items (pictures, food, skulls, etc.), or you can use each level for one category: one level for all the pictures, the other one for the food, and another level for candles and skulls.

Place the skulls and candles in front of the picture frames, alternating them: one candle, one skull, another candle, another skull. Try placing them in a way so that they do not completely block the pictures. When you face your altar, you want to be able to see the faces of your loved ones. Do not light the candles yet, as the time for this will come later when welcoming the dead to your altar. Place one or a few bigger candles in the center.

Next put personal objects of the guests or toys for the little ones close to their pictures. Then add the offerings: the bowl of salt, the cups of water, the incense holder, and the food and drinks.

Last, take some of the flowers and pull petals off. Spread the petals all over the altar, making a cross in the middle pointing to the cardinal points. Make sure to spread the petals after all other items have been set up, as placing objects on top of petals can be a bit complicated. Leave some flowers in a watered vase on your altar, so the smell of the flowers can last longer.

• ACTIVIDAD 14 •
Welcoming Your Ancestors and Loved Ones

After you have set your altar, it is time to call your dead loved ones and invite them to the celebration. This exercise describes how you can call them and invite them to your altar, expressing to them that the altar is dedicated to them. You can adapt the steps to your personal beliefs, if needed. I recommend performing this welcoming on the night of October 31.

1. Do some grounding and shielding (see page 70).

2. Have a list with all your special guests' names ready and a small white candle for each.

3. Burn some copal or incense and face each cardinal direction, raising it and offering it to each point. Set the incense back on your altar.

4. Grab a handful of flower petals and spread them from the main entrance of your home to your altar.

5. Sit or kneel down facing your altar.

6. Inhale and exhale three times, letting any thoughts pass by and trying to focus on the ritual only.

7. Light the principal candles of your altar. Here you can make a short prayer or invocation to the divinity or spiritual force of your choice.

(Great Goddess / Great God / Great Spirit / Universe), I welcome you in love and trust to this altar and festivity made in your honor and in honor of my ancestors and loved ones, those who have left before me. May this altar and ritual be in the best benefit to all that is.

If you are not spiritual or religious, the other large candles can be dedicated to light the whole altar and to guide all the spirits to the altar. Or you can skip this step and just dedicate each smaller candle to the dead loved one.

8. Light one of the small candles and call out loud the first name from your loved ones list.

9. Speak a few words welcoming your loved one:

(Name of your loved one), welcome to this altar I have set for you. Welcome to this festivity made in your honor and memory. I have missed you. Enjoy the food and water I have left for you. Have some rest, and may we enjoy the time we have together. May your arrival be in perfect love and perfect trust, until it is time to part again.

10. Raise the small candle and take a moment to welcome your loved one from your heart. Picture your loved one's face, as if you were looking at each other face to face, and feel how much you love that person. Visualize the spirit of the person arriving at your home, to your altar, happy to be there. Try remembering how your loved one used to smell, how your loved one used to talk, the tone of their voice, and how your loved one used to laugh. Then place the candle back on your altar.

11. Light another small candle and call out loud the next name on your list, repeating steps 8 through 10. Repeat until you have called all your loved ones. You can light one candle for different loved ones if you do not have a candle for each.

12. Once you have called all your loved ones, close your eyes and stay a bit of time there, sitting or kneeling. Close your eyes and visualize that your loved ones have arrived at your home, how they are enjoying the altar's food and beverages, how they are talking, laughing with each other, smiling at you. Visualize them as if they were there as any other guests at your home would be—sitting on

the couch in the living room, hugging you, talking to you, telling stories.

13. After a few minutes, whenever you feel you are done, take the copal or incense and face each cardinal direction, raising it and offering again it to each point, but going the opposite direction, starting from the last point in step 2 and finishing with the first point.

14. Take your hands to your heart and say thank you.

15. Do some grounding. Visualize any excess energy returning back to the earth.

After the welcoming, take a moment to think about what you have felt. Did you feel anything different when calling out each name? How did your surroundings feel? Did the air change? Did it feel thicker or lighter?

If you do not want to be too formal about it, you can also just light the candles and welcome your dead guests as if you were welcoming any regular guest to your home. Talk to them out loud as if you were talking with any living person and inviting them to your home, to your party. The important thing is for it to come out naturally and from your heart, to feel it.

CONSEJO

It is normal to dream of your dead loved ones during these days. Have a notebook and a pen ready on your nightstand next to your bed. If you have a dream, write it as soon as you wake up so you won't forget it. Make note of what you remember from your dream: What were your loved ones doing? How did they look? Did they say something to you? If so, what did they say?

If you do not have any dreams, do not worry. This does not mean your guests did not arrive. Your dead loved ones and ancestors are with you in heart and spirit. We all perceive things in different ways. Some people in my family do not have dreams of the dead, but they do hear noises at their home during these days. Do not be surprised if you start hearing some uncommon noises in your home after setting up the altar. Do not be afraid. The invited guests have arrived! On some occasions, I have heard sounds like clinking glasses, as if they were toasting, or sounds like steps around the house.

Maybe you do not notice anything out of the ordinary, like dreams or noises, but you start getting memories of them that you did not clearly remember before.

Chapter Five

OTHER RITUALS AND ACTIVITIES

Besides building a Day of the Dead altar at home, there are other important traditions of the Day of the Dead, such as visiting your ancestors' graves and sharing stories about them with others.

The home altar is a personal or family activity, and other activities are directed more toward the relationship with the community.

In some communities, the *ofrendas* are built around the graves after cleaning their surroundings.

In some communities, the *ofrendas* are built around the graves after cleaning their surroundings. Some communities hold vigils on the night of November 1 until the morning of November 2.

One of the biggest Day of the Dead celebrations occurs each year in the island of Janitzio, in the state of Michoacán. In Janitzio, one of the islands in Lake Pátzcuaro, the Purépecha people start their celebration with a dance, known as *la danza de los pescadores* ("the dance of the fishermen"), in which they hunt *el pato sagrado* ("the sacred duck"), which is later eaten by the people while they wait for their loved ones (Flores 2019).

In the evening of November 1, people start their journey toward the Tzirumútaro graveyard, located at the top of the island. They silently walk toward the graves of their deceased, where they later offer candles, flowers, and food placed on mats. The entrance of the graveyard is decorated with a huge arch of flowers and with a long row of candles. Thousands of lights are lit, and there are candles and torches all over the island, including the graves and on rafts in the lake. The lights and the procession can be appreciated from the lake surroundings. People stay on the graves, singing and praying, until the next day.

According to a Purépecha legend, after sunset on the Day of the Dead, the souls of the princess Mintzita and the prince Itzihuapa are present in the cemetery. The legend says that the princess Mintzita, daughter of the king Tzintzicha, and Itzihuapa, prince and heir to the throne of Janitzio, were madly in love. But they were not able to be together because of the unexpected arrival of the Spanish conquerors. Tzintzicha, the father of Mintzita, was taken prisoner by the Spaniards. Mintzita tried to rescue him by offering the treasure that was hidden in the lake. When Itzihuapa tried to extract the treasure, he was trapped by the twenty shadow guardians of the treasure, becoming the twenty-first guardian. It is said that on the Night of the Dead, the guardians rise from the lake and visit the island. Mintzita and Itzihuapa can express their love again and interact with the living.

Visiting Your Loved Ones' Graves

Visiting your dead loved ones is a way of showing them your respect and expressing your love for them. The gravesite visitation may spark a bit of fear because of movies we see or stories we hear. However, it is a solemn and quiet moment.

Take some flowers and place them on the gravestone. Take a moment and remember how they were. You can talk to them out loud and tell them whatever you need to say. Going outside and visiting the graves can also spark some questions and inspire a reflection about your own life and about death, and it can also help to deal with your grief from another perspective.

If you are not sure where the remains of your dead loved ones are located, consult with your relatives. If your loved one was cremated, you can do the same wherever the urn is located. If for some reason you do not know where the remains of your loved one are located, you can visit a place that was special for that person.

A Candle Dedicated to the Little Ones

In many communities, the souls of the children are celebrated and honored separately and have their own day.

On October 31 or November 1, take a moment to recognize and to think about the little souls, the souls of the dead children.

If there are children included in your altar, you can dedicate a moment specifically for them. If you don't know any children who have passed away and no child is included in your altar, you can dedicate a moment to the children who died as orphans.

Light a special candle for them, and next to it place some toys and candy or a beverage that they would like, such as juice. When lighting the candle, try not to think of the children with sadness, even when we may not understand why they left so early. Try thinking of them with happiness and joy, as if you were playing and laughing with them; share that happiness and joy with them when lighting the candle. From that joy, set the intention in the candle for it to guide them back to their homes.

• ACTIVIDAD 16 •
A Meditation Ritual of the Dead

This simple meditation ritual is dedicated to recognizing death as part of the eternal cycle of life and honoring your dead loved ones. Ideally, this meditation is made to be performed on the night of November 1 or on November 2, after the altar has been set. It lasts around ten to fifteen minutes. I recommend first reading it before practicing it. It may be a good idea to record your voice reading the meditation so you can listen to the audio when practicing it.

Light a white candle or the white candles on your altar and some incense. When lighting the candles and incense, you can call upon the higher force of your personal spiritual beliefs; it can be your higher self, the Goddess, the God, the Great Spirit, the universe, the Divine—whatever you feel comfortable with. Make the intention that this ritual comes from love and is made for your highest good and the highest good of all that is.

Sit down facing your altar. You can use a chair or sit on the ground. Make yourself comfortable, but try sitting with your back straight and with both feet touching the ground. Close your eyes.

Slowly inhale with your nose and feel your chest and abdomen expanding. Slowly exhale with your mouth and feel your chest and stomach contracting. Slowly inhale and exhale the same way one more time. Slowly inhale and exhale a third time. With each exhalation, release every thought that is perturbing your mind and any unpleasant physical sensation and tension.

Continue breathing, but now slowly inhale and exhale through your nose. Slowly inhale through your nose, counting from one to four. Retain the air, counting from one to four. Slowly exhale through your nose, counting from one to four. Repeat these steps, slowly inhaling, retaining, and exhaling with the same rhythm. Allow any thoughts to pass by your mind like clouds. Do not focus on any of them, do not judge them, just let them flow, but try to bring your focus back to your breathing. Keep inhaling and exhaling until you find a steady, constant, slow, and natural rhythm.

Focus your attention on your heart. Try hearing your heartbeat and identifying its rhythm. Think of how every heartbeat moves blood to your whole body, how your heart is pumping life. Feel the love you have for yourself and for life

chapter five

itself. Feel the gratitude, the wonder, and the joy of being alive. Visualize this love as a white light that emerges from your heart, moving to your head, shoulders, and legs and covering your whole body. Visualize this white light growing and expanding a bit outside of your body until you are covered by a white egg made of light. Visualize the light until you see a white screen full of light.

Visualize the white screen as a TV screen or a white painting canvas, and visualize a place in nature where you feel safe, peaceful, and loved. It can be a forest, a beach, a jungle, a garden—any natural place that you prefer. Visualize the vegetation surrounding you. Feel your bare feet on the earth. Feel the grass, earth, or sand. Feel the weather of the place. Maybe it is raining, maybe it is windy.

Walk around your safe place and explore it. Keep walking until you find a dog in your path. It is a friendly and very cute dog. It moves its tail and joyfully jumps toward you, inviting you to play. It jumps against you and then turns away, looking back at you. The dog wants you to follow it. You follow the dog for a while until both of you encounter a river. You both pause and watch the river.

Watch how the river endlessly runs and flows. Hear the relaxing sound of the flowing water. The river is the eternal cycle of life and death. It never ends; it is a constant flow. Notice how the river flows faster and stronger in some parts, while it runs slower and softer in others. See how the water creates patterns with the soil and stones and how the patterns later disappear.

You notice that in one part of the river, the water is shallow and flows more calmly. You approach that spot and introduce your feet in the water. You walk a bit, and the water reaches your shinbone and almost touches your knees. You feel the water's current and keep walking. In front of you is the other side of the river, but you can hardly see what's there, as it is covered in mist. The dog behind you is joyfully playing with some butterflies, so you leave it there. You cross the river and reach the other side.

Feel how the weather is different here. Is it colder or warmer? Is the air lighter or thicker? You walk through the mist until you are out of it. The place is very similar to the side of the river you come from, however, it somehow looks different at the same time. There is more light on this side. Everything glows. The plants shine.

You hear some voices and laughter nearby. It sounds like some people are having fun, chatting, and laughing. You follow the sound until you reach what appears to be a party. A group of people is sitting around a table surrounded by trees and plants full of flowers. There is plenty of food and drink on the table. The people notice you are watching them and turn to look at you. They smile, and you recognize some of the faces.

Although they do not invite you to their table, they are happy to see you. You notice some of them standing up and walking toward you. You are happy to see them too.

Who is in front of you? Say their names. Tell

Feel the love and the light in your heart and surrounding you.

them how you have missed them. Tell them whatever you have not been able to tell them. Express your gratitude for what they gave you when they were alive. Say thank you. Tell them you love them.

They reply. They thank you for remembering them. They let you know they are okay. They let you know all is well. They touch your shoulders and you give them a warm and long hug. They say they are happy to see you, but that it is time for you to go back. You take a moment. And when you are ready, you say goodbye, knowing it is not the last goodbye. You will see each other again.

You return to where you came from. You walk without looking back, and you hear the laughter and voices far away now. You feel the love and joy in your heart. You cross the mist. You cross the river and find the dog waiting for you. It moves its tail when it sees you. You walk together back to the place where your adventure started.

Feel the love and the light in your heart and surrounding you. Slowly, focus back on your breathing while the screen in your mind goes back to white. Whenever you feel ready, open your eyes. Feel your body and slightly move it. Visualize that any excess energy flows down through your body and returns to the earth. The earth is wise and will give it some use.

Remain sitting down, watching the candle until you feel ready. Say thank you to the higher force you previously called upon. You can leave the candle burning if it is safe and you will still be around, or you can respectfully extinguish the light.

• ACTIVIDAD 17 •

A Gratitude List Dedicated to Your Ancestors

It is said that gratitude opens a window of possibilities. With our constant troubles and day-to-day routines, we often end up focusing on our worries, on our problems, on what we want, on what we do not have, on what we cannot control. When we focus on what we do have, on the blessings of our life, we clear the way ahead and create room for more of these.

Take some time to reflect on your current life and ask yourself, "What am I grateful for?" How has abundance been manifested this year in your life? Did you have a big event or achievement in your life? Did you get a new job?

Did you graduate? Did you get a promotion or raise? Did you travel?

Think of things we usually take for granted. Do you have a roof over your head? Do you have food in your kitchen? Do you have hot water for baths or showers?

Make a list of all the things you are grateful for and dedicate them to your ancestors. Although they may have not been directly involved in all of them, they cleared the way for us. For example, the civil rights we have today are a result of our ancestors' struggles and demands.

• ACTIVIDAD 18 •
Giving Your Ancestors a Feast

Celebrating the abundance and the harvest with the ancestors is the base of the Day of the Dead. At this time of the year, we look back and appreciate how fortunate we are and the harvest of our crops, the results of our actions.

Cook some of your favorite dishes, serve your favorite drinks, and invite your close living family members and friends. Share with them what you have, no matter how small or big you consider it to be. At some point in the feast, stand up and make a toast dedicated to the dead.

You can share a special personal story about the year you have had or a story about your dead loved ones.

• ACTIVIDAD 19 •
Share a Special Story

One very special custom during the Day of the Dead is to tell and share stories of your dead loved ones. These stories are not sad but happy and sometimes even funny. It is a cheerful tradition.

Think about a story of one of your dead loved ones and share it with someone who probably does not know the story. For example, maybe you have a great story about your father, and your children never met him. Or maybe you have a very funny memory about a friend that you want to share with another friend you had in common. Once you have chosen the story, you can start the conversation by saying, "Did I ever tell you about the time when …?," or even if they know the story, you can say, "Remember the time when …?"

• ACTIVIDAD 20 •
Honoring the Ancestors of the Land

The ancestors of the land are the spirits that remain in a specific location, guarding and protecting it. These spirits once lived there hundreds or thousands of years ago. They had a strong bond with the land and their spirits remain there.

When I travel and visit a new place, the first thing I do during my arrival is take a moment and pay respects to the ancestors and guardians of the land. When entering a sacred place, like some ruins, I also ask for their blessing and permission.

Go to a place in your town or city that is very special. It can be a natural place or place with a great history. Sit down for a moment in this place, close your eyes, and after breathing and relaxing, feel the energy of the place. Picture the spirits and ancestors of the land and express to them your gratitude and your respect. You can also leave some flowers or stones as an offering.

• ACTIVIDAD 21 •
Write a Literary Calavera,
a Satirical Poem to Death

The literal English translation of the Spanish word *calavera* is "skull." However, there is a type of *calavera* that does not refer to bones. Literary *calaveras* are satirical writing compositions in verse that make fun of death and the living. They tell a story in rhyme of how death tries taking lives and exaggerate the traits of the people. Literary *calaveras* usually mention public figures or politicians. They started in the nineteenth century as mocking epitaphs and political statements.

First, think about who you are going to write about. In this case, the subject should not be dead. It can be a friend, a family member, a teacher, a coworker, or a public figure.

Then think about a special aspect or trait of the person, something that person is known for: that the person is always late, that the person is funny. Next, think about a funny way that person is going to meet death, related to their characteristic trait.

Start by writing some rhyming phrases, introducing your subject and the trait of the subject. Then introduce death as a character and set up how the subject encounters death.

For example, let's imagine I have a cousin named María who will be my subject. She is very young and is always looking at her mobile phone, barely noticing what happens around her. Her use of technology and how it consumes her attention is the trait I will use.

> While she is walking on the street,
> When she is invited to eat,
> Maria is not paying attention.
> She appears to be in another dimension.
> Death looked at her list
> And noticed Maria was missed.
> "I'm going to get her," she decided
> And went to where Maria resided.
> She yelled, "Come with me, I demand,"
> But it did not go as planned.
> Maria had not heard or seen.
> She was looking down at her screen.
> Death drew a phone from her cloak.
> "Ugh, I don't like technology," she spoke.
> Death sent her a message with a link,
> And Maria clicked on it—she didn't think.
> Death told her, "You opened the URL.
> It is time for you to come to the land I dwell."
> Maria responded, "Oh, I didn't notice it was spam.
> That makes sense.
> But . . . let's first take a selfie with my mobile lens."

Creating a Themed Day of the Dead Collage

The Day of the Dead altars are not only made at homes for ancestors and loved ones. During Day of the Dead celebrations, altars are made all around Mexican cities and towns in schools, offices, government buildings, companies, and streets. If possible, visit a local public Day of the Dead altar. If there is a Mexican or Latin-American community in your area, investigate if they created one.

If you can't find any, think about one of your hobbies or of an activity that is important to you and create a collage with the pictures of the dead people who have influenced you. If you are a music lover, make a list of all your favorite late musicians who have influenced your music taste. For instance, if you are a big fan of rock, make a list of the greatest dead rock stars who you love—Elvis Presley, John Lennon, Janis Joplin. Gather pictures or items of them and put them together in a collage. Think about how these people have influenced the subject you are passionate about and how they influenced your life. Express your gratitude to their spirits while you listen to their music and appreciate your collage. You can save your collage for years to come and add to it over time.

Pedir Calaverita

Sometimes, the Day of the Dead mingles with Halloween, as they have slightly blended with each other. When I was a child, for example, my family and I would set up our Day of the Dead *ofrenda* with my family, and we would also decorate our home with pumpkins, ghosts, witches, and other symbols of Halloween. I would then go out with my siblings and friends, and we would go from house to house asking for candy and wearing costumes.

This activity, very similar to trick-or-treating, is traditionally known in Mexico as *pedir calaverita,* "to ask for a little skull." Rumor says that it is a pre-Hispanic tradition and that it comes from when an Aztec boy didn't have anything to offer to his dead loved ones, so he painted his face and asked people for food. Some scholars, however, do not agree with this version. Another possibility is that its origin comes from when rich people used to set altars for their deceased, and people who could not afford to make their own would ask for leftovers from the rich families. The most accepted version is that *pedir calaverita* is influenced by Halloween and trick-or-treating. Nowadays, the Day of the Dead and Halloween, in some regions and oftentimes, coexist.

Chapter Six

SAYING GOODBYE TO VISITING SPIRITS

A day or a few days after the Day of the Dead festivities, it is time to say goodbye to your dead loved ones and to dismantle the altar. This is traditionally done after the Day of the Dead, between November 3 and November 8.

• ACTIVIDAD 23 •
Saying Goodbye

Start by inhaling and exhaling three times, letting any thoughts pass by, and trying to focus on the ritual only. Then, burn some copal or incense and light the candles. Similar to how we welcomed spirits in *actividad* 14, face each cardinal direction and offer the smoke to each cardinal point. Sit or kneel down facing your altar.

Make a short prayer or invocation to the divinity or spiritual force of your choice:

> *(Great Goddess / Great God / Great Spirit / Universe), I thank you, in love and trust, for your presence you have blessed us with, in this altar and festivity. I ask for your blessing so that the spirits of my loved ones return safely. May their souls be blessed by your love and guided by your light.*

Call out loud each of your dead guests' names and then speak a few words, thanking them for their visit and for their blessing and wishing them a good return and a safe journey:

> *(Names of your loved ones), I hope you liked this altar that I set for you. Thank you for coming to this festivity. It was made in your honor and memory. I hope you*

enjoyed the offerings I left for you and that you enjoyed your time at this home. May your departure be in perfect love and perfect trust, until it is time to meet again. Blessed be.

Close your eyes and visualize that your loved ones are happily leaving your home and saying goodbye to you.

After a moment, take the copal or incense and face each cardinal direction, raising it and offering it again to each point. Take your hands to your heart and say thank you. Respectfully extinguish the candles and incense.

Take a moment to think about how you feel and how you felt while saying goodbye. Did you feel anything around you? Take a look around your altar. Do you feel anything different in your home? Does the air or temperature feel different? Your home may somehow feel empty, but at the same time you think this is silly because it looks the same as before.

You probably feel a bit sad, and that is normal. It is not easy to say goodbye. Take a moment to breathe and do some grounding (see page 70).

Removing the Altar

After you said goodbye, you can now remove the items of the altar and clean the surface and space. Try offering the remaining incense, ashes, and water to the earth, burying them in your garden, a nearby field, or in your pots.

What do you do with the food? Some people eat it and share it with others. However, some other people say that after the dead enjoy the food of the altar, it loses its taste and essence. I agree with this. It is best to dispose of it, along with the flower petals, in your compost pile or following the organic waste procedures of your city, especially if you cooked something, as it is probably spoiled by now.

Candles can be burned until they are completely consumed, as the wax is not recyclable, and I suggest to not reuse the wax of these candles for other purposes, unless

Try offering the remaining incense, ashes, and water to the earth.

it is for your Day of the Dead celebrations in the next year.

Other items like the *papel picado* (if it's not too torn or wrinkled), pictures, picture frames, incense holders, candle containers, and fake food can be stored in a box or container for you to use them again next year. You can also hang the pictures or display them somewhere else in your home.

Return the glasses and bowls in your kitchen or store them with the other Day of the Dead items in case you want to use them for the celebration only.

Remembering Our Ancestors

Setting the Day of the Dead *ofrenda* is the center of the celebration. After we have the table or surface ready and we have smudged or cleansed the space with incense or copal, we add the items and call our dead loved ones and ancestors, inviting them to our altar and offering them the treats we have placed for them. When we invite our ancestors and loved ones, we do it with love and visualize them with us in our homes. Once they have arrived, we remember them, talk to them, and spend time with them.

Besides the altar, another important activity of the celebration is visiting the graves of our loved ones. Some people clean the graves and decorate them. Some leave offerings such as flowers for them. When visiting the graves, we express our respect, and most people talk to their loved ones.

Since pre-Hispanic times, the little souls, or the dead children, were celebrated separately. During the Day of the Dead, we take time to remember and celebrate them, and we give to them offerings appropriate for their age, including candy, toys, and juice.

Celebrating the Day of the Dead also includes recognizing death as part of the eternal cycle of life. While honoring our ancestors and loved ones, we also end up reflecting on our origin, on our present, and on our future. We think about things of our life that died, such as situations or people who may not have died but are no longer parts of our life. We also recognize our own mortality and think about what we are going to leave to the world when our time for us to leave comes.

We remember our ancestors: of blood, of space, or of spirit. The people we descended from. The people who made an impact on the land we live in. The people who

influenced our spiritual beliefs and practices. People who have passed away but whose lives changed our world.

Everything has a cycle, and the celebration of the Day of the Dead also comes to an end. After the celebration, between November 3 and November 8, we give a farewell to our ancestors and dead loved ones, until the time to greet them comes again the next year.

CONCLUSION

The time to celebrate the dead has passed. We have remembered our loved ones. We have spoken with our relatives and friends about those who have left before us. We prepared our home for the special guests, we welcomed our loved ones, we set an altar for them, we dreamed with them, and we spoke with them. We offered them food and drinks. We recalled a lot of sweet stories.

We cried and laughed. We told them all the important things that have happened in our life since they left.

The time to say goodbye came again. It was not a "goodbye forever," though. It was a "see you soon." Nothing is finite: everything comes and goes. Everything has a cycle. We will have the opportunity to celebrate the dead again next year, but now is the time to focus on the present moment and to celebrate life, to celebrate our lives every day.

The popular tradition sees the Day of the Dead as a moment when our ancestors and dead loved ones visit us. However, it is my personal belief that it is not exactly a visit. They have never left us. During this time of the year, the veil between the living and the dead becomes thinner, so we feel them closer. They are always with us, in our hearts and in spirit. We can remember them and honor them throughout the year, and the best way of doing so is to live the best lives we can.

Let's celebrate that we are alive, in honor of those who have died and blessed our life. Let's enjoy the life we inherited from our ancestors, as we would not be here now if it was not for them. Be grateful for what we have had and of what we have today. Love, care for, and respect the people who are alive and present in our life, as we never know when the last opportunity will be.

The best way to honor our ancestors is to every day try to become a better person, creating a better version of ourselves and a better version of the world. We often think of our ancestors and other people who came before us as if our state will remain constant: the ancestors and us, the dead and the living. However, we will be somebody else's ancestors one day, either of blood, of place, or of spirit. Even if we do not plan to have children of our own, our actions today create possibilities for the people of tomorrow. Our ancestors had their ancestors when they were alive, and so we are the yet-to-be ancestor of our land and of our world. Let's start protecting and cherishing our land and community today and creating a better world for the people of tomorrow.

Blessed is life. Blessed is death. Blessed is the cycle of life and death.

Merry meet, merry part, and merry meet again.

What is remembered lives.

GLOSSARY

ACTIVIDAD: Activity, exercise.

CALABAZA EN TACHA: Candied pumpkin, emblematic dessert dish of *Día de los Muertos*.

CALAVERA: Skull. Can also refer to the literary satirical poems of someone meeting death. A *calaverita* is a "little skull."

CALAVERA DE AZÚCAR: Sugar skull. Edible and colorful skulls made of sugars decorate the Day of the Dead altars.

LA CATRINA: A satirical representation of death created by the late nineteenth- and early twentieth-century artist José Guadalupe Posada and later renamed and painted by Diego Rivera. Originally called *la Calavera Garbancera* (satirical for "elegant skull").

CEMPASÚCHIL: Traditional flower of the Day of the Dead with strong yellow-orange color and strong sweet smell. Its scientific name is *Tagetes erecta*, also known as the Mexican marigold.

CONSEJO: Tip or advice.

COPALERA: Holder and burner for the copal or incense, in form of a chalice.

LA LLORONA: The Weeping Woman, famous Mexican legend of the spirit of a woman who cries for her children.

MAGUEY: Agave plant. Used to make alcoholic drinks.

MARIPOSA: Butterfly.

MICTLÁN: The Aztec underworld.

LOS MUERTOS: The dead.

glossary

OFRENDA: Offering, altar.

PAN DE MUERTO: Bread of the dead. Traditional food for the Day of the Dead, sweet bread with the shape of body remains.

PAPALOTE: Kite.

PAPEL PICADO: Tissue paper of different colors with cut out shapes.

QUETZALCÓATL: The Feathered-Serpent (*quetzal*, a colorful bird; *coatl*, "serpent"). One of the most important deities in Mesoamerica. Known as Kukulcán in Mayan culture. Deity of the wind and of life. Related to Venus and the morning and the creation of humans.

LA SANTA MUERTE: Folk saint of death.

VELA: Candle.

XOLO: Short for Xoloitzcuintli. The Mexican hairless dog, one of the most ancient dog breeds.

BIBLIOGRAPHY

Books and Journals

Conaculta. 2006. "Patrimonio de la humanidad: La festividad indígena dedicada a los muertos en México" [World Heritage: The Indigenous Festivity Dedicated to the Dead in Mexico]. *Patrimonio cultural y turismo* 16:13–22. https://www.cultura.gob.mx /turismocultural/publi/Cuadernos_19_num /cuaderno16.pdf.

De la Garza, Mercedes. 1999. "La muerte y sus deidades en el pensamiento maya" [Death and Its Deities in Mayan Thought]. *Arqueología Mexicana* (November/December): 40–45. https://arqueologiamexicana.mx/mexico-antiguo/la-muerte-y-sus-deidades-en-el-pensamiento-maya-0.

———. 2014. "El carácter sagrado del xoloitzcuintli entre los nahuas y los mayas" [The Sacred Nature of the Xoloitzcuintli among the Nahua and Maya]. *Arqueología Mexicana* 125 (January/February 2014): 58–63. https://arqueologiamexicana.mx/mexico-antiguo/el-caracter-sagrado-del-xoloitzcuintli-entre-los-nahuas-y-los-mayas.

Domingo Olivares, Leticia. 2016. "Prácticas discursivas en la lengua nahuatl de Cuentepec, Morelos y su influencia en la educación" [Discursive Practices in the Nahuatl Language from Cuentepec, Morelos and the Influence in Education]. Bachelor's thesis, Universidad Pedagógica Nacional. http://200.23.113.51/pdf/32869.pdf.

Hutton, Ronald. 1996. *The Stations of the Sun: A History of the Ritual Year in Britain.* Oxford: Oxford University Press.

Johansson, Patrick. 2003. "Días de muertos en el mundo náhuatl prehispánico" [Days of the Dead in the Pre-Hispanic Nahuatl World]. *Estudios de Cultura Náhuatl*

34:167–203. http://www.historicas.unam.mx
/publicaciones/revistas/nahuatl/pdf/ecn34/678.pdf.

———. 2003. "La muerte en Mesoamérica" [Death in
Mesoamerica]. *Arqueología Mexicana* 60 (March/April):
46–53. https://arqueologiamexicana.mx/mexico
-antiguo/la-muerte-en-mesoamerica.

Lomnitz, Claudio. 2006. *Idea de la muerte en México* [Death
and the Idea of Mexico]. Mexico City: Fondo de
Cultura Económica. Kindle.

Matos Moctezuma, Eduardo. 2010. *La muerte entre los
mexicas* [Death among the Mexica]. Mexico City:
Tusquets. Kindle.

———. 2013. "Los mexicas y la muerte" [The Mexica
and Death]. *Arqueología Mexicana* 52, special edition
(October): 18–20. https://arqueologiamexicana.mx
/mexico-antiguo/la-muerte-y-sus-deidades-en-el
-pensamiento-maya-0.

———. 2014. *Muerte a filo de obsidiana: Los Nahuas frente
a la muerte* [Death on Obisdian's Edge: The Nahua
in Front of Death]. Mexico City: Fondo de Cultura
Económica. Kindle.

Noguez, Xavier. 1996. "El culto prehispánico en el Tepeyac"
[The Prehispanic Cult in the Tepeyac]. *Arqueología
Mexicana* 20 (July/August): 50–55.

Pacheco, Leobardo. *Aprende y pinta los dioses Zapotecos* [Learn and Paint the Zapotec Gods]. Oaxaca: Instituto Nacional de Antropología e Historia Oaxaca, n.d.

Paz, Octavio. 1950. *El laberinto de la soledad* [The Labyrinth of Solitude]. Mexico: Fondo de Cultura Económica.

Perdigón Castañeda, J. Katia. 2008. *La Santa Muerte, protectora de los hombres.* [Santa Muerte, protector of men]. Mexico City: Instituto Nacional de Antropología e Historia.

Ríos, Guadalupe, Edelmira Ramírez, and Marcela Suárez. 1997. *Día de Muertos* [Day of the Dead]. Mexico City: Universidad Autónoma Metropolitana.

Vaughn, Bobbie. 2001. "Mexico in the Context of the Transatlantic Slave Trade," *Diálogo* 5, no. 1 (March): 14–19. https://via.library.depaul.edu/cgi/viewcontent.cgi?article=1060&context=dialogo.

Westheim, Paul. 2014. *La calavera*. Mexico City: Fondo de Cultura Económica. Kindle.

Exhibitions

Arte popular funerario y ritual [Popular Funerary and Ritual Art]. 2018. Aguascalientes, Mexico: Museo Nacional de la Muerte, December 2018.

Visiones de la muerte en el mundo [Visions of Death in the World]. 2018–2019. Mexico City: Museo Nacional de las Culturas, October 2018–February 2019.

Web Sources

Alper, Tim. 2016. "Life after Death—The Beguiling World
    of the Korean Jesa Ceremony." Korea.net. January,
    2016. https://www.korea.net/NewsFocus/Column
    /view?articleId=131596.

"Conoces el significado de los elementos de una ofrenda
    de Día de Muertos?" [Do You Know the Meaning of
    the Elements in a Day of the Dead Offering?]. 2019.
    Instituto Nacional de los Pueblos Indígenas. October
    23, 2019. https://www.gob.mx/inpi/articulos
    /conoces-el-significado-de-los-elementos-de-una
    -ofrenda-de-dia-de-muertos.

"La Danza de los Diablos; patrimonio afromexicano en la
    Costa Chica de Guerrero" [Dance of the Devils; Afro-
    Mexican Heritage in the Costa Chica of Guerrero].
    2019. Secretaría de Cultura. June 5, 2019. https://
    www.gob.mx/cultura/es/articulos/la-danza-de-los
    -diablos-patrimonio-afromexicano-en-la-costa-chica
    -de-guerrero?idiom=es.

"La fecha de hoy y el calendario mexica" [Today's
    date and the Mexica calendar]. N.d. *Arqueologia
    Méxicana.* Accessed December 29, 2020. https://
    arqueologiamexicana.mx/la-fecha-de-hoy-calendario
    -mexica/la-fecha-de-hoy-y-el-calendario-mexica-113.

Flores, Karla. 2019. "Día de Muertos en Janitzio" [Day
    of the Dead in Janitzio]. Revista Central. October 31,

2019. https://www.revistacentral.com.mx/que-plan
-revista-central/exposiciones/notas/dia-de-muertos
-en-janitzio.

Frankovich, Jessica. 2019. "Mexican Catholicism: Conquest, Faith, and Resistance." Berkley Center for Religion, Peace & World Affairs. March 22, 2019. https://berkleycenter.georgetown.edu/posts /mexican-catholicism-conquest-faith-and-resistance.

Islas, Brenda. 2019. "Día de Muertos, una tradición muy viva" [Day of the Dead, a Very Vivid Tradition]. Noticias ONU. October 31, 2019. https://news.un.org/es /story/2019/10/1464731.

Mata Loera, Martha E. 2020. "Día de muertos en un país con culturas diferentes" [Day of the Dead in a Country with Different Cultures]. Gaceta. Universidad de Guadalajara. November 2, 2020. http://www.gaceta .udg.mx/dia-de-muertos-en-un-pais-con-culturas -diferentes/.

"Ocotepec celebrará Día de Muertos, tradición reconocida por la UNESCO" [Ocotepec will celebrate Day of the Dead, tradition recognized by UNESCO]. 2014. Instituto Nacional de Antropología e Historia. October 31, 2014. https://inah.gob.mx/en/boletines/1683 -ocotepec-celebrara-dia-de-muertos-tradicion -reconocida-por-la-unesco.

"Orígenes profundamente católicos y no prehispánicos, la fiesta de día de muertos" [Origins Deeply Catholic and Not Pre-Hispanic, the Day of the Dead]. 2007. Instituto Nacional de Antropología e Historia. November 1, 2007. https://www.inah.gob.mx/boletines/1485 -origenes-profundamente-catolicos-y-no-pre -Hispanicos-la-fiesta-de-dia-de-muertos-2.

"El origen del pan de muerto y las variedades regionales actuales" [The Origin of the Bread of the Dead and the Current Regional Varieties]. 2019. Instituto Nacional de los Pueblos Indígenas. October 25, 2019. https:// www.gob.mx/inpi/es/articulos/el-origen-del-pan-de -muerto-y-las-variedades-regionales?idiom=es.

Romey, Kristin. 2017. "This Hairless Mexican Dog Has a Storied, Ancient Past." *National Geographic.* November 22, 2017. https://www.nationalgeographic.com /news/2017/11/hairless-dog-mexico-xolo -xoloitzcuintli-Aztec/.

Vela, Enrique. 2014. "Miccailhuitontli y Huey miccaílhuitl." *Arqueologia Méxicana.* 2014. https:// arqueologiamexicana.mx/mexico-antiguo /miccailhuitontli-y-huey-miccaihuitl.

"Xandu', Día de Muertos zapoteco del Istmo de Tehuantepec" [Xandu, Zapotec Day of the Dead of the Istmo de Tehuantepec]. 2018. Instituto Nacional de los Pueblos Indígenas, October 26, 2018. https://www

.gob.mx/inpi/agenda/xandu-dia-de-muertos
-zapoteco-del-istmo-de-tehuantepec.

"Xantolo Xalapa 2019, tradición e identidad" [Xantolo
Xalapa 2019, Tradition and Identity]. 2020. Xalapa City
Council. October 19, 2020. https://ayuntamiento
.xalapa.gob.mx/home/-/blogs/xantolo-xalapa-2019
-tradicion-e-identidad/maximized.